ULSTER IN THE AGE OF SAINT COMGALL OF BANGOR

Michael Sheane

D1336275

ARTHUR H. STOCKWELL LTD.
Torrs Park   Ilfracombe   Devon
Established 1898
www.ahstockwell.co.uk

British Library Cataloguing-in-Publication Data.
A catalogue record for this book is available
from the British Library.

Arthur H. Stockwell Ltd., bear no responsibility
for the accuracy of events recorded in this book.

Dedication: To Derek, Helen and Family

By the same author:
Ulster & Its Future After the Troubles (1977)
Ulster & The German Solution (1978)
Ulster & The British Connection (1979)
Ulster & The Lords of the North (1980)
Ulster & The Middle Ages (1982)
Ulster & Saint Patrick (1984)
The Twilight Pagans (1990)
Enemy of England (1991)
The Great Siege (2002)

ISBN 0 7223 3599-7
Printed in Great Britain by
Arthur H. Stockwell Ltd.
Torrs Park   Ilfracombe
Devon

Contents

Chapter 1 *Magheramourne, Early Sixth Century* 5

Chapter 2 *The Sixth Century Papacy* 12

Chapter 3 *Celtic Spirituality* 19

Chapter 4 *A Short History of Bangor Abbey* 26

Chapter 5 *The Concept of Kingship* 33

Chapter 6 *The Bangor Antiphonary* 39

Chapter 7 *The Nature of Society* 45

Chapter 8 *"A Remnant of Chaos"* 52

Chapter 9 *The Mystery of the Cross* 59

Chapter 10 *Slaves and Workers* 65

Chapter 11 *The Mother of God* 73

Chapter 12 *Sex and Marriage in Ancient Ulster* 79

Chapter 13 *Hunting, Fishing and Seafood* 85

Chapter 14 *Another Look at the Gaels* 92

Chapter 15 *The Celtic Supernatural* 98

Chapter 16 *How Comgall Read the Gospels* 104

Chapter 17 *Trade and Transport in Sixth Century Ulster* 110

Chapter 18 *The Sacraments* 116

Chapter 19 *Learning and Literature* 122

Chapter 20 *Comgall and the Risen Christ* 125

Select Bibliography 127

Chapter 1

Magheramourne, Early Sixth Century

Saint Patrick had been and gone in Ulster when Saint Comgall was born in AD 517, perhaps into a pagan family in the little Gaelic kingdom of Laharna on the north east coast of Ireland. Comgall no doubt had heard about the fame of Patrick, the Apostle of Ireland, and perhaps he wished to emulate what may have been his favourite preacher. The Pope at Rome lay many hundreds of miles away across Europe and into the Italian peninsula — it was and still is an Italian organization claiming to represent the true faith. The Pope claimed to be head of the Catholic Church, which had embraced much of Europe by the fifth century, the age of the decline and fall of the Roman Empire. The Pope was anxious that little communities like that of Magheramourne in Ireland should always receive the Catholic Church, in an age when the popes were holy and honourable, not like that of their medieval counterparts.

Comgall may have studied the Bible, either as a curious pagan or as a young Christian, if he was born into a Christian family. Modern Magheramourne lies about five miles from Larne, seat of the ancient Laharna kingdom, and about twenty miles from present day Belfast. The Antrim coast was well known to the young saint as he travelled the length and breadth of Laharna. Here he would come across anchorites or solitary monks, worshipping Christ on the shores of County Antrim. Today Magheramourne has only a small population, a bit like the ancient settlement. It may have had a chapel or a small monastery, but to be sure this early Christian settlement looked to the power of spiritual Rome. It is not known how pagan the sixth century townland was, but it is certain that the young Comgall was an important member of the community, either as a pagan or as a devout Christian. He was probably literate and as a monk would have made copies of the Scriptures for Bangor monastery, his great achievement.

The ancient kingdom of Ulster, based at Armagh, had fallen when

5

Comgall started to worship: Saint Patrick had made Armagh the Primatial See, and Comgall would often visit the see. He looked towards Armagh as seat of the Catholic Church in Ireland. Magheramourne itself was part of the wider political confederacy in Ireland, based at Tara, north of Dublin. At Magheramourne Comgall tried to convert what remained of the druid colleges or universities in Ireland. Magheramourne, lying on the shores of Larne Lough, looked towards Belfast Lough in its efforts at trading with communities lying on the west coast of Britain. Through these western ports all sorts of Christians may have reached the north east of Ulster. Missionaries, before that of Rome, had penetrated reaching Armagh before the advent of Saint Patrick.

The kingdom of Ulster or the Ulaid had fallen by the fifth century, and the primatial see was erected on the ashes of a once united province. Magheramourne lay fifty miles from Armagh — Comgall may have often made the journey to Armagh Cathedral, said to have been built by Patrick. Magheramourne had its own chieftain who looked up to the rí or king of Laharna or Larne. This was the pagan tradition, and the rís survived the expansionist forces of Comgall's Roman and Catholic Church.

The ancient kingdom of Dalriada may have reached the shores of Larne Lough by the sixth century, not only in the age of Comgall but also the age of Columba of Derry and Iona. Comgall may have travelled north to Benbane Head and to Dunseverick, capital of Dalriada, which expanded across the Sea of Moyle or North Channel into Argyll to be known as Scottish Dalriada. The popes had their eyes upon the little Gaelic kingdoms like that of Magheramourne, where the Gaels lived in daub and wattle huts, with thatched roofs. However by the age of Comgall the Roman Empire had fallen and the Ulster pressure of population from the west of Ulster was being laid upon regions like that of Magheramourne.

Man had inhabited Magheramourne from earliest times, and the tribes looked out across Larne Lough to the kingdom of Island Magee, as it is popularly called. The druids, bards and poets had dominated the life of early Magheramourne, and they competed with Comgall's Church, in representing religion and political truth. The seasons came and went at Magheramourne — Beltane the start of the Celtic New Year in May, Imbolc or the start of Spring in February, Samain the start of Summer in May and Lugnasad the start of the Celtic Autumn in August. Magheramourne was a totally agricultural society, governed by the chiefs or large farmers. It was also a violent place, and the Gaelic warriors competed with one another to control the area. Like Columba, Comgall may have been one of these warriors, eventually being received into the Catholic Church. Early Catholics at Magheramourne tried to absorb pagan traditions in order to make conversions to the Church easier for the rís, druids, and of course for the ordinary warriors and farmers.

The sun shone down upon Magheramourne, an important deity,

worshipped by the druids or magicians. Comgall had declared that like Christ he wanted to save sinners, so that they would inherit the kingdom of God. The pagan Gaels somehow took to the faith, and Comgall's ambition to establish Christianity in North Down would come to fruition. The coast of North Down was visible from the banks of Belfast Lough, and Comgall may have made the journey by currach or small boat, sailing from one of the ports of North Down. He established the monastery of Bangor in the mid sixth century, again building upon the foundations of Saint Patrick. Magheramourne looked out across Larne Lough to the crannogs or lake dwellings, built as fortifications: rubble was dumped into spots on the lough shore upon which were erected island dwellings. These dwellings were either wholly, largely circular or oval islands in lakes. They were usually built of dumped layers of peat, brushwood, heavier timbers, stone and soil, and many were originally surrounded by a palisade or fence of closely knit vertical timber and round wood parts. They survive today as free-clad islands in lakes or as stone cairns and earthen mounds. Larne Lough may have had a number of crannogs, together with the lakes on Erne, Lough Neagh, Strangford Lough, Lough Foyle and Lough Swilley. They served a variety of functions. Some may have been defended farmsteads, where people could work in safety. Some crannogs were royal residences, where kings lived for a number of months in a year. They may also have been used by craftsmen. Crannogs were also used as refuges in wars between rival kings and chiefs. The water-logged nature of crannogs has meant that rich, complex, archaeological deposits are often preserved. Ancient plant remains, seeds, beetles, animal bone are also there. These crannogs have mostly been discovered in the nineteenth century. As lake levels were lowered, crannogs would be found and evidence of early settlement could be obtained. By 1886 there were 220 crannogs to be found in Ireland as a whole. Many of them date from the early medieval period (AD 500-1200), beginning in the late sixth and early seventh centuries. Numerous crannogs can be found in Antrim, Fermanagh and Down.

It is not known the precise reason the Gaels built crannogs. They could be occupied either for a matter of months or for years. Some of them were built and abandoned very quickly. There is an interesting crannog at Craigywarren in County Antrim, a small site. Most crannogs were occupied during Saint Comgall's lifetime. Many of the crannogs have remained uncovered, as they were swamped and covered in the waters. These tend to be found in smaller lakes, probably because sites like this in the lakes of Fermanagh were too windswept. This may also have been true of Larne Lough . Occasionally they could be found in deeper water. Crannogs vary in size — about 10-15 metres in diameter to 30-40 metres across. They could also be used as fishing platforms. It took a number of months to build a crannog, and it could also be a dangerous task. Little is known of the number of houses that made up a crannog, and there is little evidence of sophisticated dwellings. Crannogs were reached by way of a causeway, from the crannogs to the shore of a lough or lake. Where there was no causeway the crannogs were reached by a boat.

It is not likely that Comgall inhabited a crannog, but they may have been used as an ecclesiastical function. The monks would be safe from attack by hostile pagans or rival monasteries. The diet of the crannog would have been based on milk, eggs, grain and meat produced in the farmland around the crannog. Deer, fish and wildfowl could have been trapped in the lake. Cattle grazed in the surrounding fields; other livestock were also grazed. Crannogs were sometimes built adjacent to good arable and grazing ground. The crannog dwellers were independent in domestic crafts. They made bowls, carved tubes, slave-built buckets, spoons and ladles and occasionally pieces of decorated wood. Textiles were also made in a small number of crannogs. There were also iron workings. In the early medieval period some crannogs were attacked by rival clans and tribes. There were also royal crannogs, the residence of powerful kings, and if Larne Lough boasted crannogs then the Rí or King of Laharna was an occupant of one of these remarkable structures that numbered about 1,200 in the whole of Ireland. Many of the crannogs may date from the arrival of the Milesians or Gaels in Ireland, somewhere between 1000-350 BC, coming from a cradle in the Alps, also a site of lake dwellings. If Larne Lough or even the shores of Belfast Lough boasted crannogs they would have been the site of monastic and other communities. They may have been sacked in the early Viking invasions of the north east of Ulster, for modern research seems to point to an earlier date other than AD 795 for the arrival of the Vikings in Ireland/Ulster.

Comgall himself was a Gael, a Celt, though he may not have regarded himself as an Irishman, for in those days there was no national state. The island was ruled in theory by the Ard Rí or High-King, who was a civilized tribal "emperor". He was the "King of Ireland", and his subjects numbered about half a million, mostly Christian by Comgall's time. Men like Comgall were living in the tradition of the Catholic Church. Certainly Comgall's Christianity must have been based on the Bible, but the role of the Pope by the sixth century was decisive. The popes at Rome had now claimed that the Roman Church was the father of all other Churches either in communion with or separated from the holy see at Rome. The origins of monasticism go far back into antiquity. Other civilizations, for example Mesopotamia, boasted monastic and zenobite communities, people who would take themselves into an isolated spot to worship the deity, Christian or otherwise. Women were also encouraged by the Roman Church to become "brides of Christ".

Perhaps there were men at Magheramourne who may have educated the young Comgall, as well as being educated by the monks. Comgall's

Catholicism was to be evangelical, for he accompanied Saint Columba (AD 521-597), a good friend, on his mission to the Picts of northern Scotland. Comgall cleansed his mind of worldly ambition, and from a young age he had it as his aim to establish a monastery and educate youth in the beliefs of the Catholic Church. It is not known why Comgall chose Bangor, County Down, as his site for a monastery, rather than Magheramourne, County Antrim. Perhaps the Gaels of North Down were still a little pagan.

The shape of Ulster is the product of the recent Ice Age, which by 11,000 BC had spent itself. Its contribution to Ulster are the smooth-shaped U-valleys in central Donegal, the Mourne Mountains of south east Down, and the drumlins that stretch from Loughs Strangford and Carlingford in a wide sweep through Monaghan, Cavan and south Tyrone as far west as Donegal bay. This was the Ulster of Saint Comgall, geographically little different to the geography of the province (nine counties) today. Donegal was the birthplace of Saint Columba, and Derry the site of his great monastery. The Donegal of today is the same as the Donegal of Comgall and Columba. The mountains of Donegal rise up from the Atlantic, and the River Foyle empties into that great ocean. Comgall must have been aware of the many tribes and kingdoms that made up not only Tirconnell (Donegal), but also the rest of Ulster, particularly the Ulster of the Ulaid (the united Ulster kingdom).

In his own territory Comgall would travel the paths and roads of present day County Antrim, walking or riding in a chariot to the Glens of Antrim and to Dunseverick in North Antrim, seat of Dalriada. These trips would have taken a few days to complete, and it is certain that the young Comgall had an intimate knowledge of not only County Antrim, but also the sister kingdom in County Down (Del Fitach), particularly North Down. Bangor was his great achievement, founded in AD 558. The Antrim plateau rises up from the Sea of Moyle or North Channel, and meets the shores of Lough Neagh. Lough Neagh was known to Comgall as The Great Lake. It is the largest freshwater lake in the British Isles, and it is in size the extent of a small Irish county. On the east coast of County Antrim lies Larne Lough, about five miles in length, stretching from Larne to Ballycarry. Not only was it the site of Comgall's early career, but it was also the scene of the Viking invasions and was known as Ulfrek's fjord after the Norse sea king who overthrew the tribes of Laharna, and who also subjected Dalriada, Irish and Scottish. The little ports of the Antrim Coast traded with Scotland and its Western Isles, and Magheramourne and Larne have a long history of intercourse with not only eastern England, but with the Scottish kingdoms. Both Antrim and Down shared the same waters, the waters and tides of Belfast Lough, a seat of Gaelic Christianity from ancient times. From Magheramourne it took only a few hours to row or sail to North Down, and the great abbey-to-be of Bangor in County

Down. Down also boasts Strangford Lough, scene also of the Viking invasions of the ninth century.

As in modern times there were many settlements in the Strangford region, but most of all are the larger and beautiful Mourne Mountains that dominate south east Down. All its slieves were there in Comgall's time, and he must often have visited Downpatrick, travelling from Magheramourne or Bangor along the trading roads and paths. Alternatively he could have sailed from Magheramourne down Belfast Lough and into the Irish Sea, anchoring off the south east coast of Down, bringing his Catholic faith with him. As scenery goes it is difficult to choose between the Mountains of Mourne and the Antrim hills and coast. In Comgall's day the mountainous regions of Ulster were full of legends, telling the history of Ireland (or Eirinn). Downpatrick is one of the great patrician centres, and little communities like Magheramourne looked up to the ancient site of Patrick's first church in Ireland. He was mostly an Ulster saint, as had been Columba, founder of Iona.

The littoral that stretches from Belfast to Ballycarry was well inhabited in ancient times and Comgall must have travelled the road to Gaelic Belfast, or sailed up the coast, past present day Whitehead, Carrickfergus and Newtownabbey, reaching the little kingdom of Belfast. Comgall travelled into central Ulster, and here he fell in love with the great Sperrin Mountains, famed for its forests. Now he was in the kingdom of Tir-Owen or Tyrone (the land of Owen), the land of the great O'Neill clan, now presumably in the sixth century entirely converted to Christianity. The lakes of Erne lay further to the south west and here the ancient druids frequented the forests of the lakes. In the sixth century Ulster was deeply wooded; perhaps the earliest churches and monasteries were made out of timber, but it is more likely that the original Bangor Abbey was made out of stone. The great rivers of Ulster (the Bann, the Foyle, the Lagan) were famous for their fish. Magheramourne on the east coast was ideally situated to fish the waters of Larne Lough, the North Channel and the Irish Sea.

Among the sites of the Antrim Coast lay Rathlin Island, inhabited by man from earliest times. The journey to this ancient monastic centre took a day by ship and about the same time by road.

The first men in the Magheramourne area were hunters and fishermen, as were the inhabitants of nearby Laharna or Larne. The Gaels of Magheramourne and Bangor valued their independence of political Rome, which had ceased to exist in the West since the mid fifth century. Here on the edge of Europe the great ecclesiastical age had taken root from humble origins.

The Vikings were to sack the altars at Magheramourne and Bangor along with the overthrow of the Catholic Church at ancient Armagh. The Church appreciated the tales of olden Eirinn, and gradually after the fall of Rome the High-Kingship could claim that the Kings of Ireland ruled an "Irish" island. Irish nationality and its roots form an interesting story. Suffice to say that there were about 250 different tribal kingdoms or tuatha in the whole island, all by the sixth century having their saints, but amongst these Patrick, Columba and Comgall remain famous. By Comgall's day the provinces of Eirinn had taken shape — Ulster, Leinster, Meath (later disbanded), Munster and Connaught. Presumably our saint travelled widely in them.

Chapter 2

The Sixth Century Papacy

By the sixth century the Papacy had been well established, despite the barbarian invasions of the fourth and fifth centuries in Europe. It is useful to look back at the progress of the Papacy from its inception, said to date back from sometime after the birth of Christ. The Bible tells us nothing about the position of the Pope in the primitive Church. Bishops, deacons and priests are mentioned, but there is no authority for the establishment of the Papacy, or an infallible leader of the Church Universal. The word "Catholic" is not used. It is probably true that Christ meant that some sort of earthly organization should lead the Roman Empire. At the last supper or holy communion Christ broke bread and drank wine, saying that man should do this in remembrance of him. It is certain that Comgall believed in some sort of version of the Eucharist or mass, perhaps like that of the Anglo-Catholic Church today.

During the first century the Papacy was a persecuted organization. All sorts of crimes were blamed on the Christians, for example the burning of Rome. Comgall must have had a very poor opinion of the Roman imperial system. Comgall looked back to the infant Papacy of the first century, probably regarding Peter as leader of the Church. Some authorities think that Linus was the first Pope, but the Catholic Church specifically looked to Saint Peter as the first Pope of the Church. Christ had given Peter a commission — "Thou art Peter and upon this Rock I shall build my Church". Christianity had spread from Palestine and the Near East in the first century. Its progress was remarkable, and in the age of Comgall, the miracle of the Church continued to be performed in sixth century Ulster. Europe was now dominated by the pagan barbarians.

Saint Peter, and Saint Paul were crucified at Rome for their beliefs. The Romans thought that Peter and Paul were hostile to the state, for they denied the divine nature of the emperor or caesar, even though Christ had said that it was necessary to "render unto Caesar the things which were

Caesar's". Comgall did not challenge the role of the state in Ulster. He accepted the status quo, but the king or rí ruled the tribal region or tuatha. It was necessary to obey the rí or king in order to have a form of belief in the Catholic system. The sixth century Papacy was a sophisticated organization. It could look back at six centuries of Catholicism, and many popes.

By the first century the Roman state had turned itself into an empire, and under this system Peter and Paul laboured and made conversions. Rome was a very materialistic and wealth-based civilization, and people wanted something more tangible than a belief in a divine emperor. The Scriptures predicted that Christian leaders would be persecuted by the state for the sake of the kingdom of God. In Comgall's age this was still possible in Ulster even though the druids had been discredited. There was also the risk of a resurgence of paganism or kings that were hostile to the Catholic Church. The first century, unlike the sixth century, was a mainly pagan world. Both Peter and Paul had made journeys and missions in the efficient communications systems of the Roman world. It was inevitable that they would reach Rome and establish the Church in the great city of the emperors. First century Rome was a city of magnificent walls, and it boasted great buildings and palaces. For Comgall Emain Macha or Armagh, seat of the former Ulster kings, was a modest affair. Peter must have regarded the Roman state as the Antichrist but future Protestant generations were to regard the popes of the Catholic Church as the Antichrist.

Comgall had escaped being brought up under Roman Britain, with a possible invasion of Eirinn or Ireland by the aggressive Empire. The Church produced the New Testament and Paul is the most prolific contributor. Peter had only a small say, despite being claimed as the first Pope by the present day Roman Catholic Church. The Bible says that Christ is present if a few people are gathered together in order to worship. It says that Christ ordained some sort of "democratic" Papacy to lead the Church. Hatred of invasions of the nations under the Roman Empire was foremost, not beliefs in doctrines and dogmas, however useful these would be in the life of the faith. As Abbot of Bangor Abbey Comgall received all the beliefs of the Church. He was not a rebel or a martyr like the popes of the first century; some lost their lives for their beliefs. It is not known where the first century popes ruled from, but they probably held sway in a small chapel or church in the city of Rome. It was not long until the Christians started to write about the faith, Peter amongst them. The Old Testament was the foundation of the New Testament, and Christ's coming and crucifixion was predicted (and necessary) for the devout souls of the first and second century Church. In his epistles or letters Peter does not mention that he was the first Pope or that Christ had used the word "Pope". However the Catholic Church teaches that Peter had an implicit command from Jesus, and that future generations would regard him as the first Pope of the Church.

The barbarian invasions of the fourth and fifth centuries ended in the defeat of the West. Under pressure of the barbarian invasions, the seat of the Empire had moved to Constantinople in the East, and here the Byzantine Church had established itself, eventually breaking with Rome to become the Greek Orthodox communion. Comgall may have regarded Peter as the first Pope. Certainly by the sixth century devout souls looked to the Pope as foremost bishop in the Church. Christ perhaps had meant that there should be a Church, for had he not twelve apostles, an earthly organization, and did he not give verbal commission to Saint Peter, a worldly man, who denied Christ. The Church was a "fallible" organization, becoming "infallible", for Pope Pius IX in 1869 defined the doctrine of Papal infallibility.

Throughout the Roman world the rule of bishops was seen as a defence against heresy, as well as in the Church of Saint Comgall. The rule of bishops was recognized by the Pope as essential for salvation. Irenaeus wrote in his "treatise against the heresies" that it was up to the individual to find truth. By the sixth century Comgall's Church was governed by bishops, despite the original monastic flavour of the Celtic or Gaelic Church. The Papacy seems to have been established by the mid 150s. Heresy may have entered the Church of Comgall, but heresy seems to have been an entirely Roman and Continental phenomenon. The popes soon wanted to compile a list of bishops of Rome, a process that may have started about AD 150. From the start the bishops of Rome presided over a divided Church for there were heresies and the position of Constantinople, which had established its own brand of Catholicism. By the third century the see of Rome appears to have been acknowledged as the foremost see in Christendom. Comgall saw the birth of Papal Rome, but he has left us no writing about the position of the Irish Church. His eyes looked East to Constantinople and Rome.

Europe was divided into many petty kingdoms. In Ireland there were the Celtic tribes, in England the Anglo-Saxons, the Franks in France, the Visigoths in Spain, the Lombards in Italy, while the rest of Europe fell under East Rome. The popes started to quarrel amongst themselves, and anti-popes emerged. The popes regarded Ireland in the same light as they did the barbarians, despite the age of art and learning. It was Europe's greatest desire that it should one day achieve the unity it had at the time of the Empire. Pope Hormisdus was reigning when Comgall was born in AD 517. He was later made a saint alongside Comgall. He was an Italian, aristocratic and rich. He married before ordination and had a son Silverius, later himself a Pope. Hormisdus was a great peace maker, and reigned from 20 July AD 514-523. He was a demolisher of heresies and ended the long Arcadian schism (AD 484-519), between East and West.

By now the rift between East and West, for the faith, had become serious. Christ had meant his Church to be united in the face of the materialistic world. The Church of Rome has outlived many heresies, more challenging to the Catholic Church than Protestantism.

Comgall, as far as it is known, was never married. If he was a converted pagan, he may have given in to the lusts of the flesh. As a monk he would have lived a very holy life, and as Abbot of Bangor Abbey in North Down, he would have led a celibate life. It was the barbarians' ambition to overthrow monastic establishments like that of Bangor, and to put to death men like Comgall, and to steal the treasures of the Church.

By the sixth century in Ulster and Ireland an early Renaissance had started. In Europe beautiful churches and chapels had been founded and one must look at the art in the chapels and cathedrals of the Eternal City of Rome. It is thought that Christianity had reached the Rome of the caesars by AD 30. Christians were not permitted to worship in public until the fourth century. In Ulster at this date there may have been small pockets of Christians arriving in Eirinn and Ulster via the sea ports of the west coast of Britain. First century Rome was a city of great buildings and Comgall's monastery of Bangor was small in comparison with the Continental achievements. Christians were eaten by the lions in the amphitheatres, and they believed in the power of Christ and his saving word, as they met their deaths.

Peter died at Rome under the emperor Nero. The early Christians met in secret houses where holy communion or the mass was celebrated. Unlike in Ulster the Christians went in fear of their lives. This had been predicted by Christ, who wanted Christians to sacrifice themselves for the sake of the kingdom of Heaven.

Roman art is more colourful than Gaelic or Celtic art. The churches, chapels, cathedrals and monasteries in West Rome were alive with colour, and the atmosphere is Roman and Catholic. From the first century Christians made images of Christ and the Virgin Mary, along with the saints. Most believers were illiterate, and images were useful in explaining the faith. The Papacy was all for colour, and Bibles (for use of priests only) were beautifully copied by hand, and they too, were renowned for their colour. Christianity may have reached Rome through a variety of ports. In Ulster art was the prerogative of the Church, and saints like Comgall proclaimed their belief in images to explain the faith. The Bible stipulated that graven images were pagan symbols of non Christian faiths. To some extent the Church borrowed its art from the pagan Gaels. It was easier to make conversions using images of Christ and the Virgin Mary. Images were made of the Latin and Greek saints and holy men. Comgall is almost certain to have used images during his attempts at conversion of remaining pagans at Bangor and North Down. The sixth century popes were learned and arty people, along with the upper classes of Irish society.

It is not known whether the Irish druids of magicians used images of the gods. They were sun worshippers until the coming of the Catholic Church. Excavations in Ulster and at Rome have through the decades shed a little light about the artistic and ritualistic Christianity of the age. The Romans, both East and West, revered icons or pictures of the saints and the Virgin Mary. Ireland is a mine of information about the early Celts and also about the establishment of Christianity or "the way", as it is called by the early Church fathers. The early Christians at Rome (and Ulster) may have appreciated the art and learning of the Empire, but they wanted Rome to be a Catholic and imperial place, that looked back to the early first century and the coming of the apostles Peter and Paul to the region. Irish copies of the Bible are full of colour, as witness the beautiful Book of Kells (sixth century), now in the care of the library at Trinity College Dublin.

According to the German historian Gregorvin: "until the time of Leo I in the fifth century, the Chair of Peter had not been occupied by a single bishop of any importance", for in the early days the Church was mainly concerned with the hope of survival in a hostile environment. Christians were hated by the Jews, a conflict that was not to be seen in Ulster in Comgall's day. Christians however would not enlist in the army, thus casting doubt on their loyalty as citizens. As in Rome, Christians in Ulster were mainly drawn from the lower classes who had no wealth and were politically victimized. Christ had come to save the poor in spirit. After the death of Marellinus in AD 304 there was no bishop in Rome for four years and at this date the Church does not seem concerned about who should be Pope. However by the time of the emperor Constantine the Church was recognized and was bequeathed land and privileges. Christians started to quarrel amongst themselves about the nature of the Catholic faith, in an age when heresies had started to come to the fore.

The Bishop of Rome became a great landowner and civic leader. At Comgall's Bangor this may also have been the case, for the Irish monasteries were wealthy organizations; chalices, crosses and plates were made out of silver and gold, not to mention the costly statues of Christ and the Virgin Mary. Comgall's sixth century Church was not in the position of the Church of Rome, about planning how to survive. This did not happen until the invasions of the Vikings in the ninth century (some say the Vikings may have reached Antrim and Down as early as the fourth century). Papal morals were becoming lax in the sixth century. The Pope was more like a potentate than a holy bishop. The Church was also examining the nature of the faith, and great Councils of the Church had taken place, for example the Council of Chalcedon in AD 451. In Ulster the rí or king ruled the land, holding authority from the Pope. Abbeys like that of Comgall's Bangor became powerful political organizations, which held themselves aloof from Rome. During the age of the Abbey of Bangor the monastery was favoured by the local king and both abbey, kings and aristocracy looked east to Rome and its popes.

Comgall did not like corruption in the Church. He had studied under Saint Fintan of Clonenagh, County Laois. He was reputed to have cured a blind man by pressing saliva into his eyes. Comgall also spent some time at Lough Erne, County Fermanagh, where he was subjected to a tight regime. It was now that he moved to Bangor in North Down. The monastery of Bangor attracted thousands of monks, amongst them being Saints Columban, Gall and Moluay. He allowed himself only one meal per day, and many of his miracles concerned food. He died in Bangor on 11th May, AD 603. By the sixth century the authority of the Pope was greater than that of a Council, but the average Gael loved the Pope, which meant "abba" or father in the Latin. However the Church was also concerned in healing rifts between the various Catholic communions. The sixth century Papacy was a more constitutional body than the present day Roman Catholic Church. In the sixth century the Catholic Church was close to the original fathers of the first century. The Church, as today, is a relatively young organization. The Church venerates the great fathers of the latter day Roman world, and the monasteries were great repositories of wealth. Other centres of Christian tradition like Alexandria were older than that of Rome, so that they could also claim to be the original centres of the faith. Peter had chosen Rome as a result of its unique situation as capital of the Roman Empire in the first century.

From Rome missionaries may have reached the shores of Larne Lough and Belfast Lough. News about the faith perhaps to start with was made by word of mouth, to be written down in the New Testament at a later date. The demise of political Rome had not spelt the end of Rome as the city of the popes. Christianity transcended nationality and allegiance to the tribe. God had appointed Peter and his successors to lead the world. The forces of Hell would not prevail against the Papacy and its many popes. The sixth century Papacy boasted many millions of souls, firstly connected with paganism and the druid gods, both in Ulster and the Roman Empire. Comgall was no Pope's man in the modern sense. He was a rigorously independent evangelist and monk, and would have condemned later Papal policies. He was a simple Christian, waiting to convert the tribes to the Catholic Church, and to have them remain converted.

The Gaelic or Celtic Church was to produce many saints — Declan of Ardmore, Patrick of Ireland, Bridget of Kildare, Finnian of Clonard, Brendan the Navigator, Gildas the Wise, Ciarin of Clonmacnoise, David of Wales, Comgall of Bangor, Columba of Iona, Kentigern of Glasgow, Columban of Luxeil, Dympia of Gaheel, Fursey of Peronne, Aidan of Lindisfarne, Gall of Saint Gall and Colman of Lindisfarne.

Let us also document the popes that reigned in Comgall's age, and whom he venerated as Vicars of Christ: Saint Hormisdas, Saint John I, Saint Felix IV, Dioscorus (anti-pope), Boniface II, John II, Saint Agapitus,

B

Saint Silverius, Vigilius, Pelagius I, John III, Benedict I, Pelagius II, Saint Gregory I, Sabinian, Boniface III. All the popes looked west to the edge of the Atlantic, and to the Celtic world, and to Ulster and its many monasteries erected along the coasts, in mountains, and along its rivers. Ulster was distinct from Scotland, to whom Saint Columba had brought the faith, with the Pictish mission of the late sixth century. These popes, as Christ would have made allowance for, had all the weaknesses of the flesh, but still the sixth century Papacy survived in an age in Europe that had brought the barbarians to the gates of the Pope's city of Rome.

Chapter 3

Celtic Spirituality

Anyone that has visited the Antrim coast and the Glens of Antrim, Northern Ireland, must be struck by the beauty and silence of the place. The coast road runs from Larne in the south to Cushendall in the north and hugs the coast of the Sea of Moyle or North Channel.

Comgall was himself perhaps not aware that early man had come across the Sea of Moyle to settle in the Larne region. Excavations in the early part of the twentieth century have discovered a "Larnian" or Stone Age culture. Comgall was certainly aware of the atmosphere of the early Gaelic or Celtic Church in the region that stretches from Magheramourne on the banks of Larne Lough to Fair Head, where the Mull of Kintyre in Scotland looms only thirteen miles away. In the last century interest has been aroused about the facts concerning the Celtic Church in an age of violence in Ulster. People are turning to the beliefs of the primitive Church in order to find some sort of fulfilment. Some books have appeared since the 1970s about the character of the Gaelic Church, which claims to be very close to the faith of the apostles.

It is very hard to define the word "Celtic" — it obviously points to all the tribes or nations that made up the "Celtic" peoples in the British Isles — the Britons, the Welsh, the Scots and the Irish. Initially some of these nations made up the Gaelic Church, looking to Armagh in Ulster for leadership, but also acknowledging the role of the Pope. Modern man in Ulster has perhaps discarded some Reformation ideas, that the Pope is Antichrist. In Comgall's day the Antichrist was perhaps epitomized in the person of the barbarians who had taken over Rome in the mid fifth century. The Antichrist was also represented in the person of the druids, but they had been discredited by Columba and Comgall. Gaelic Christianity taught that Christ had become flesh and dwelt amongst us. In the chapels of the Magheramourne and Cushendun area (Dalriada), images in great colour adorned the churches, but the Gaels did not consider themselves as making

19

graven images. The spirit of God dwelled in the churches, and also at Armagh the Primatial See. For Comgall Christ was the only mediator between God and man, and the Virgin Mary took second place. Comgall believed that Christ had existed and that he was crucified and buried so that the sins of mankind and the Roman Empire should be forgiven. This Christ was a young man, perhaps about thirty, who had taught the new faith or "the way" in Palestine, and who meant that Christianity should eventually encompass the whole world.

The Gaelic Church was a chaotic organization. Armagh was merely a centre rather like Tara, and the archbishops ruled over a confederate Church. Comgall must have made the journey to Armagh on many occasions, there to have an interview with the Primate. Celtic spirituality has to do with the idea of the Irish Church in particular. The Gaels considered themselves as representing the one true Church. It is true to say that there were many Celtic Churches. The word had become flesh and dwelt amongst us. This was the faith that had been taken across the Sea of Moyle in the fifth century, to become established in Scottish Dalriada and Argyll. Comgall may have believed that the Second Coming of Christ was near. At Magheramourne and Bangor he grew up in the evangelical tradition. Perhaps from an early man he had ambitions to build upon the work of Saint Patrick. The monastery epitomized the atmosphere of the Church. In many respects the monasteries were governed as one body, as the Gaelic Church became organized in the sixth century.

At the Sea of Moyle the young Comgall may have imagined Christ walking upon the waters, for Comgall loved the Scriptures and the miracles that Christ performed. Christ had been crucified by the Romans. He had been sentenced to death by Pilate, but he also said that he could find no fault in Jesus. Comgall would have had mixed feelings about spiritual Rome, but by the sixth century the persecutions of a previous age had ceased. The waters of the Sea of Moyle reminded our saint of the great flood recorded in the Bible. Water had a great significance for Christianity, for it was used in baptism. The Antrim coast was cold, with its bright sunsets in summer, which could also be seen at Iona in the Western Isles. Comgall may have travelled up the coast to the monastery at Rathlin Island, there to celebrate mass and to thank God for all the blessings of the Catholic Church.

Comgall knew that Christ would some day judge the living and the dead. There were many graveyards in the kingdom of Laharna and Dalriada. Peter and Paul believed in the Second Coming, and they may have believed that it would be in their lifetime. God would bring peace to his followers and to the first three centuries of pagans at Rome. Along the coast of Antrim visions of the Virgin Mary may have been seen, as well as apparitions of Christ. Irish Christians had established a Primatial See. This was the work of man and his Christian traditions, condemned by some of the Protestant Churches today. Comgall learned about the kingdom of Israel, and its favoured place in history. He wanted to lead the pagans of Scotland to repentance and to believe in the Catholic system.

Early man had occupied most of the coastal regions of Ireland, as well as occupying the Antrim coast and Larne region. It is not known at what precise time that the Creation took place, but Comgall could imagine the volcanoes of the coast, and also the volcanoes of the Scottish coast. Early man had brought the gods with him, but Comgall and Columba built upon the Church of Patrick, where Christianity was based upon the Bible and the traditions of the Church. Christ had come to prepare the way to paradise. The Church of Comgall was a civilized product of the Celtic world. The monks had definite conceptions of God, and believed that he was a powerful spiritual being. He dwelt along the Antrim coast and in North Down where Celtic Christianity reached a zenith in Ulster. Early Christianity is part of the heritage of the Irish Church today; Catholic, Anglican and Presbyterian. Presbyterians tend to shut themselves off from the person of Comgall, but it is certain that many images of him were made as Christianity gathered pace in Eirinn and Ulster. We can understand the spirituality known to Comgall by basically studying the Bible and the writings of the Church fathers. In the beginning God created the heavens and earth. The hand of God was at work in the striking headlands of the Antrim coast and in the imposing Mourne Mountains. Comgall, like his contemporary Columba, copied the Scriptures, and in so doing he tried to understand the will of his Maker. Comgall looked out across the North Channel to Scotland, believing that God had created this in a single day. He would travel north to the Giant's Causeway disbelieving the mythology surrounding it, that it was a creation of a giant. God had completed his creation in six days, and on the seventh day he rested from all his work. Comgall, as described today, was a fundamentalist, and there must be sound reason why he, and other monks of great intelligence took the word of the Bible literally. Today most Catholics, Anglicans and Presbyterians do not take the Creation story literally. A liberal and symbolic interpretation of the Creation is popular — but will this always be so? Modern archaeology has proven that cities described in the Bible actually existed, and there is abundant evidence that Christ was an actual person. Where was the Garden of Eden? Was it an eastern or western phenomenon? Do all religions have their Garden of Eden?

The tale of the Garden of Eden shows how God had originally created man, and how Eve had tempted Adam, so that man knew sin and shame. Comgall would have understood that it was essential to believe the Bible and the traditions of the Roman Church in order to get into Heaven. God had also made the stars and the solar system, the Sun and the Moon that shone down on Comgall's monks. As Comgall travelled in the Glens of Antrim as a pagan youth or young convert the presence of God would be felt. All this was God's work, taking place at an unknown date in history. Celtic spirituality was basically no different from the spirituality of other Catholic communions. The Bible was there to unite Christians and for men like Comgall to interpret for the literate and illiterate.

The Bible tells the story of the kingdom of Israel and about its Messiah who had come to save the world and the nations. Comgall was a gentile and a Catholic, looking both to Rome and to Palestine as a rule for the faith. Comgall taught that all were equal in the sight of God, and that the world had been created for man. God had anointed kings, he had favoured the rí or king of the kingdom of Dalriada (Irish and Scottish).

There is not much room given to the Creation story in Genesis, but it must surely be the most important fact known to us in the Bible, along with the coming of Christ, the Jewish Messiah. There is not enough evidence about Celtic spirituality, for much useful material may have been destroyed in the Viking invasions. This of course deals mostly with political history, but the Bible and writings of men like Saint Patrick provide us with useful pointers and facts. It is not known how many Christians lived in sixth century Ulster, and there is no evidence to show that there was any great pressures of population; emigration from south-west Ireland occurred in the fifth century when the Dal Riata tribe moved north to north Antrim, later to be known as the kingdom of Dalriada. There may have been about 20,000 Gaels in County Antrim, all eventually putting their faith in the Catholic Church. In Europe the population was more dense, even though the barbarians had overthrown the Church.

It is perhaps true to say that the coastal regions of Ulster were more densely inhabited than the interior of the province, this making Patrick's and Comgall's task much easier. Comgall was sure that God would eventually evangelize all of the Gaels in Ireland, but it must be remembered that he was a northern saint, trying to please Armagh, the Primatial See. A conversion had taken place if the person firmly believed in Christ and the primacy of the Pope. It is also certain that Comgall took literally everything that was in the Bible, and also firmly believing the writings and strictures of the Church fathers, Roman, Greek, Gaelic (or Celtic). Comgall was all for punishing Gaels who would not acknowledge Christianity as a civilizing force.

In Europe the Church had been associated with the civilization of political Rome from about the second or third centuries, and there was also the civilization of Israel, which hoped to preach the word of a single God. Comgall may have regarded the Jewish God in the form of a man, for it was said in the Bible that God created man in his own image. He was a super intelligent being, the creator of everything. He had given commandments to Moses outlining what was to become the Catholic faith. God was a God of the desert and oasis, and he had existed before the advent of time. Our saint was aware of the Judaism and Christianity of the

Near East and Palestine. To there he looked for inspiration, for had not Saints Peter and Paul come from the warm regions. Peter was probably aware of the situation in Ulster, and some believe that the early evangelists had reached Ireland, anticipating the arrival of Saint Patrick by many centuries.

The island of Ireland had the same geographical make up as the Ulster and Eire of today, but it lay on the western fringe of the Atlantic Ocean, and was hard to reach, and in the case of the Roman Empire, to conquer or civilize. This was left to the Middle Ages when the English kings asserted their authority mainly in the coastal regions. The Gaels believed that they could save what remained of civilization in Europe. The Irish monasteries were more sophisticated than their European counterparts, for they had been sacked and some destroyed during the reign of barbarism on the Continent. It is said that the Irish saved civilization, notably in the missionary journeys of Saint Columban, not to be confused with Columba of Doire (Derry) and Iona in the Western Isles of Scotland. The Gaelic or Celtic Church was subordinate to the Uí Neill hegemony in the north of Ireland. The Uí Neill kings were descended from the Connachta in the fifth century. They carved out kingdoms for themselves in the west of Ulster and in the Irish midlands. Their chief enemy was the Ulaid, which Comgall had learned to venerate. The Ulaid ruled an overkingdom or confederation of kingdoms which dominated the north and its subject peoples. The capital was at Armagh or Emain Macha, and the Ulaid was not conquered until the mid fifth century. The authority of the Ulaid was eventually confined to an area east of the Bann and Lough Neagh. The Ulaid held out in this reduced territory with the coming of the Normans in the twelfth century. This territory was also not a united kingdom but rather a confederation of peoples of different origins which did not become an overlordship until the tenth century.

The ancient kindred of the Ulaid ruled a territory equivalent to the diocese of Down and Connor. These, the Dal Fitach or Cruithin, were organized into two subkingdoms, Dalriada in the diocese of Connor and the Ui Echach Coban in the diocese of Dromore. Authority alternated between the Cruithin and the Dal Fitach until the tenth century when the Dal Fitach overthrew their rivals and monopolized the kingship. After the fall of the Ulaid in the fifth century the territory from the west of Tyrone to the Bann and including south west Ulster were settled by many subject peoples of different races and allegiances. The most important of these peoples were the Airgialla who were composed of three main groups: the Hi Truirti claimed descent from an ancestral figure Fiachra Tort, son of Colla Uais. Their territory stretched along the western shores of Lough Neagh from the Blackwater to the Moyola River. The second group was known as the Fir Li, whose territory stretched along the west bank of the Bann to the sea. The third tribe was the Ui Fiachrach Ardsratha occupying the southern and western parts of Monaghan, a portion of South Tyrone and Fermanagh to the Erne lakes. At a later date the Ui Chreni thainn were also formed into an area west of Lough Erne. The third and last great grouping of the Airgialla were Fir Rois, Ui Meith, Fir Chili and the Mugdorna, who were probably a subject people. It is certain that Comgall had an intimate knowledge of the little tribes and kingdoms. There were the Cianactha, in an area about Glenn Gainin in north central Derry, all these little kingdoms professed the faith of the Catholic Church by the sixth century. Now at an early date the kingdom of the northern Uí Neill was also divided into three groups ruled by three brothers, Conall, Eogan and Enna. The family of Enna achieved little and fame rests with the Cenel Conaill and Cenel Eogain, who originally settled the poor lands of Donegal and Inishowen. From Ailech Comgall learned that the tribes had spread eastwards and southwards. In Comgall's time the territory of the Cenel Eogain comprised the Raphoe district, Ailech, the royal seat, the plain to the east of the Foyle estuary, the valley of the Faughan and Bodoney in Tyrone. In the sixth and seventh centuries they expanded rapidly and encroached upon the lands at Derry and Tyrone held by the Airgialla peoples, the Ui Mac Uais, Fir Li and Ui Tuirtri. These tribes, spread out on a canvas in central Ulster, were directly subject to the Uí Neill overking and the High-King at Tara.

The Cenel Eogan expanded south and brought under their control the present day County Tyrone and the ecclesiastical capital of Armagh. The Cenel Eoghan kept a house at Armagh. They tried to consolidate their position in the north, and the young Comgall must have observed the various movements and quarrels amongst the tuatha as threatening the unity of the Catholic Church in Ulster and in the rest of the island of Ireland.

The spiritual tradition laid great emphasis upon unity, for only in unity could Christ's Church establish peace in Ulster.

The expansionist spirit however of the northern Uí Neill dynasty spelt some degree of unity in the early Irish Church. Armagh with its monastery and cathedral represented the Celtic spirit of Christianity in Eirinn or Ireland. The Bible, Comgall said, supported all efforts at unity in the Church, which guarded matters of faith and doctrine, presided over by the Pope. The doctrine of the Trinity represented the unity of Christendom and Churches like that of the Gaelic one in Ulster. There were three persons in the Trinity presided over by one God — father and son and holy spirit.

There was also the figure of the Virgin Mary who also exhorted the Irish tribes to unity, even to subject themselves to a Tara monarchy. The history of the Church, so all these tribes came to understand, was the story of the Pope's mission to rule the Church and to send out missionaries to countries like Ireland that had only been slightly influenced by the Empire and the Roman Church.

Comgall, a believer in unity, exhorted the kingdom of Ulster (the Uí Neill) to look to the Roman Church as a model for faith. Only by believing in the Roman Church could the average Christian find salvation. Only in believing in the sonship of Christ and in the mother figure of the Virgin Mary, could Ulster take its place amongst the great Christian nations of the world, for example the Italians and the Iberians (Spanish and Portuguese), not to mention England which by the Middle Ages was a great Catholic kingdom.

Chapter 4

A Short History of Bangor Abbey

The main task that Columba set himself was the training of monks that would bring the word to the post civilization world of the Roman Empire, for the barbarians had attacked the frontiers of Rome in the fifth century, successfully sacking the city. Unlike his contemporary and friend Saint Columba, Comgall wanted to educate youth, and in so doing he based his teaching upon the Bible, and the writings of the Church fathers. The Christian life was a great challenge for the Gaelic youth of Bangor Abbey and its associated monasteries that made up the present day counties Antrim and Down. The students travelled from many parts of Ireland to be taught by the highly devout Saint Comgall.

The sixth century was an age full of temptation for youth. In the secular world morals were questionable, and the monastic life meant that temptation had to be resisted. In many respects it was an age like our own, that lives in the shadow of the overthrown European empires of the twentieth century. There is a new arrival upon the scene — the growing power of the United States, and the decline of Soviet Russia.

Comgall founded Bangor Abbey when he was about forty-one years of age, after much soul searching and reading of the Scriptures. It is not known why the saint chose North Down as his headquarters for presumably County Antrim was closer to his heart, and his beloved Magheramourne, where he was born in AD 517. North Down and Bangor had intimate intercourse with the tribes of Western Scotland, and presumably the monks of Bangor set sail in their currachs across the Irish Sea from Belfast Lough to found monastic centres in the Western Isles, along with the missionary efforts of his friend Saint Columba. Religious education for youth started perhaps at about fourteen or fifteen and literacy was essential to keep the edge of resurgent paganism in the person of the druids. The monks started making beautiful manuscripts that were circulated amongst the monastery's sphere of influence or "paruchia". For Ulster youth of the sixth century the conversion of the pagan tribes was a great challenge; they also assumed that the already-existing Christian tribes remained loyal to Saint Columba and the Roman Church. Comgall's Bangor was a combination of great Christian centres, which competed with monasteries in Britain, in the Western Isles, part of the Dalriada sphere of influence. These monasteries were extremely busy by the time of Saint Augustine's mission to the British in AD 597. The sixth century mind was extremely conscious of the spirit of evil — the Devil — in society. The various heresies the Church tried to combat, were inspired by the Devil, and Comgall was personally aware of his struggle with the powers and principalities of the age.

Christ was relatively a young man by the time of the crucifixion about AD 32. The monks that would leave Bangor's shores would be about eighteen or nineteen or older, sailing south into the Irish Sea, and perhaps heading for Rome to have an audience with the Pope; others, as we have seen, set down roots on Scottish and English shores, establishing their monasteries. The Bible was Comgall's personal God — in the Scriptures was recorded the history of the world as Christians should understand it. The early Roman state had seen the Antichrist, but the Christian tradition was alive in the East, at Constantinople, East Rome, as it was called. In Ulster the Gaelic communion took root, as important and as colourful as the Latin communion. The Gaelic Church was of course subordinate to the Latin rite. From its very inception the Irish churches (for there were many churches and monasteries) were like the High-Kingship, a confederate organization. Comgall believed that "small was beautiful" and that diversity in worship meant some kind of spiritual unity. In this he differed with the Roman Church which was based at Rome and later in the East at Constantinople.

Youth was the lifeblood of Comgall's Abbey, for in the sixth century life expectancy was short. Youth figures largely in the Bible, for were not Adam and Eve a young couple that rebelled against the law of God. In the Bible — and in Ulster the young man is portrayed as a warrior worshipping the God of Israel.

Comgall, like his friend Columba, was quite likely a Gaelic aristocratic warrior, who eventually turned to God and Christ, regarding his way of life contrary to the law of the Bible and Church. In the Old Testament the warrior Jew conquers and slays for the sake of the kingdom of Heaven. In Ulster Comgall exhorts his young men and believers to be prepared to kill the pagan and unbelievers for sake of the kingdom of God. Comgall quotes the Scriptures and within the walls of Bangor Abbey he and his band of men prayed for peace in the land of Ulster, for above all else Comgall believed in Christ's dictum that it was essential to turn the other cheek to aggression. Youth exhorted the kings, for youth was exposed to temptation, just like the first Adam and the first Eve. However it is true to say that Christianity made progress in Ireland as the

27

result of land and property given to the Church by the local kings or rís. Comgall was well used to living under the kingships of ancient Ulster. However conversion of the rí did not automatically mean the conversion of the kingdom or tribe. Like Patrick, Comgall was living in an age that saw the decline in paganism generally since the fourth and fifth centuries.

Comgall understood all the laws regarding Gaelic kingship. There were three grades of kingship; rí or rí tuaithe, the king of the local tuatha or Gaelic kingdom. There was the ruiri or great king, who as well as being king of his own tuatha, was also the overking of many tuatha. Lastly there was the rí ruirech or "king of the overking", who is identified as the king of a province. Also, although not mentioned in the law tracts, there was the Ard Rí or High-King. The basic rí had very limited functions, for he neither owned the land or enforced public or private justice except in such matters as revolt against himself, offences against aliens and questions that involved the other tuatha. Nor was the rí a great landowner of tribal territories, for these were owned by the free families (cenel, fine) within the kingdom. However the rí was prominent in regard to external relations. He made peace and war, and conducted inter-tribal relations. All this Comgall had to take into account in regard to his relations with the tribes, as he evangelized the tuatha.

There were also the heads of the free families. There was the aire tuíse or tuísech who was representative of his aristocratic group or cenel. The classical law tracts, although not later that the eighth century, presumably recorded life in Ireland from an early date. All these institutions, e.g., a kingship, were to be challenged by the Viking invasions of the fourth to eighth centuries. By the sixth century the independent legal position of the tuatha or petty tribal kingdoms was being steadily eroded by the greater overlords.

The peasant regarded the rí, and the priest and bishop, as guardians of the Irish way of life. There had been little violence between pagan and Christian, and violence in the island can be dated back to as early as the fourth century when the Norse decended upon the Ulster monasteries, arriving in the fourth century via the north coast of Ireland and by Lambay Island on the east coast, just north of Dublin, which became a Viking colony until the demise of the Norse in 1014. Comgall leaves us no writings about the fourth century date for the coming of the Norse, but modern research has shown that by the sixth century the Vikings had colonized and farmed many locations, not only in the south of Ireland but in Ulster, probably dating back to the excavations at Ulfrek's fjord or Larne Lough on the north east coast of Ulster. The Vikings may have plundered Bangor Abbey by the sixth century, sailing up Belfast Lough, and running up the beaches, dragging their boats behind them. The Norse of course had heard about the great monastery of Bangor and it was their intention to sail down the Atlantic and into the North Channel or Sea of Moyle to put the

Christians of the Abbey to death. For Bangor the age of the Antichrist had come and was not to end until the final defeat of the Vikings at Clontarf, north of Dublin, in 1014. It is undoubtedly true that Bangor may have existed as some sort of religious foundation before the Comgall Abbey (AD 558-602). The annals of Ulster state that one Laelagius had visited Ireland in AD 431 some years before Saint Patrick's period of slavery at Slemish in mid County Antrim.

The annals of Ulster, also called the annals of Senait Mac Manus, were penned at Upper Lough Erne. The original compiler was (Cathal) Maguire, who died of smallpox in 1498. The rest of the annals and histories of Ireland date back to the eleventh century. Before this one is dependant upon hearsay and tradition in order to bring life to the kingship grades and the life of Comgall's Bangor. According to some sources monasticism in Ireland was in decline by the sixth century, others that it was a period of reform. Certainly throughout Ireland in the sixth century, Christianity was expanding.

History records that Comgall was ordained a deacon and priest by Bishop Lugidin, a man of deep learning and spirituality. Comgall was later to earn the title as one of the great founders of Irish monasticism. It was said that "Christ loved Comgall, the Lord". Above all else, for the modern Catholic, Bangor Abbey is a symbol of the Marian devotion of the primitive Irish Church. Much of the early history has been lost with those terrible Viking cruelties, and because of population reasons, the Vikings spread out from Scandinavia.

Comgall soon gathered together a following of monks, their numbers unknown, maybe they were drawn from the tribes in the Magheramourne area or locally in Bangor. Their devotion to scholarship became well known and Bangor could match anything that the monasteries of the south of Ireland could boast. It is likely that the Bangor monastery carried out intimate relations with Columba's monastery at Iona. It would have taken a number of days for Comgall and his followers to reach the great Iona monastery. Iona of course was not part of the Bangor "paruchia" or monastic sphere. The monks sailed north out of Belfast Lough and into the North Channel, passing Island Magee in the Laharna kingdom, then veering up the Antrim Coast on their way again due north, on their way to the Western Isles. The North Channel and the Atlantic were stormy seas and many sailors and monks may have been lost in the great waves. By the time Comgall reached Iona, Ireland was out of sight of eye. Now Comgall was greeted by Columba, who however was banned from returning to Ireland for political and religious reasons (he had copied one of the gospels against the will of the owner). The High-King had banished him from Ireland, but in actual fact Columba is said to have returned to Ulster on a number of occasions in spiritual and political missions.

Comgall also established a church on the island at Tiree, but it never

29

reached the population of Columba's Iona. The world of Comgall was a world without women or nuns. The Bible had stated that it was up to them to carry the gospel to the nations. The Papacy was a male preserve, and the sixth century was an age also of the male anchorite. Although Christ was a man, his mother was the Virgin Mary. The Church stated that women had a definite role, and they had to believe in the Pope and the Bible, and in the Virgin Mary as a mediator between man and God.

On Iona Comgall watched Columba's monks tend the cattle and sheep and bring in the harvest. The monks of Iona and Bangor were basically farmers. At Bangor the monks prayed for peace in the land and for rich harvests, both on the land and upon the sea. The monks of Bangor fished in the deep waters of Belfast Lough and the Irish Sea, landing their catch upon the beaches, and sailing about in their currachs. Christ had said that he was a fisher of men, and Saint Peter and the other apostles followed their master. The Virgin Mary is portrayed in the gospels as the mother of God, but unlike her divine Son, she did not perform any miracles, at least in her earthly existence. On the little island of Tiree, statues were perhaps set up to Christ and the Virgin, but it is certain that by the sixth century the importance of Mary was emerging in the Church Universal. On Tiree Christians could take themselves away from the world and worship Christ and the Virgin Mary in their own way.

However Tiree probably fell under the Iona monastery, and lay about ten miles from Columba's foundation. Tiree lay out in the Atlantic, and as well as a haven for monks it also had a wild life. The Atlantic waves rolled onto the shores of Tiree, and the monks would dream about Bangor, more peacefully situated on the coast of North Down. Tiree was also known as the "land of corn", where the rain fell both day and night. Demons were also thought to inhabit the island, but the spirit of Christ drove them away.

Bangor was probably bigger than the monastery of Derry in north west Ulster, and it is possible that they competed with each other for the leadership of monasteries in Ireland. Travelling to Derry from the shores of Belfast Lough took a couple of days by sail, or twice this by land. Inland Ulster was inhabited by hostile tribes, some of them still pagan; it was safer to travel by sea.

Comgall was to bequeath to Ulster a long line of illustrious abbots who governed the Bangor monastery. The abbots immediately following him were Beogna (606), Sillan (610), Fintan (613). During the abbacy of Fintan, Bangor was burned either by the early Viking raiders or in a dispute between rival monasteries. Maelrubha, a Bangor monk and later its abbot, founded Applecross monastery in Rossshire and visitors to the Scottish Highlands will find many places dedicated to him. Saint Cathach founded the monastery of Lismore in AD 635, which became a great monastic light, while Saint Molua founded Drumsuat in County Monaghan in Kyle in

County Leix. However Columban was the most famous of all the sons of Bangor, along with the missionary, one Gall. Columban had twelve companions, and Comgall would have been proud of him. Columban set out from Bangor in AD 589 and later established the monasteries at Anagray, Luxeuil and Fontaines. He established his last monastery in the Empire at Bobbio in Italy.

It is said that the Irish saved civilization during these barbarian years in Europe, and the Pope had much to thank Comgall for, after laying the foundations of Irish Christian civilization in Europe. Saint Gall made his way to Switzerland where he laboured amongst the Alemanni until his death in AD 645. Although the monastery of St Gall was not directly founded by Irish monks, it became a great centre of Irish influence, its music school under Moengal, an Irishman, became the wonder and delight of Europe. There were close links between Bangor and Bobbio in Italy, according to the seventh century book, the Bangor Antiphonary. The book is believed to have been taken from Bangor to Bobbio in the ninth century to avoid its destruction by the Vikings.

The Bangor Antiphonary is now preserved in the Ambrosian Library in Milan. In the Antiphonary is the Celtic exhortation — "Draw night and take the Body of the Lord". The golden age of art and learning at Bangor came to an end at the beginning of the ninth century, when it was devastated by the Danes. In the raid of AD 824 Comgall's tomb was desecrated. In this period many of the monks were slaughtered. A dark age reigned until 1124 when Malachy became Abbot of Bangor. Instead of the rule of Saint Comgall at the monastery, the rule of the Augustinians now took its place. Saint Malachy died in the arms of a friend in 1148.

Bangor became the seat of the diocese of Down, and as such it remained until 1144 when Pope Innocent issued a bull restoring the position of Saint Patrick. The tower of the present abbey church dates from the late fourteenth century and formed the central tower of a large and fine Augustinian church. The history of Bangor Abbey is poorly documented between the thirteenth to the mid sixteenth century. The monastery was dissolved in 1542, at which date William O'Dorman was abbot. The possessions of the monastery were surrendered to the Crown. The abbey remained empty for some time.

The abbey church was repaired in 1693, and extensive repairs were carried out on the abbey church in 1833 at a cost of £950. Bangor Abbey was reopened in 1917, and the population continued to grow. The organ now occupies a place at the west end of the nave and the abbey is an abbey parish. The present day inhabitants of Bangor have perhaps little knowledge of the long history of their abbey. The early medieval period shines out, when Bangor was dubbed "the light of the world".

The abbey's roots are Catholic and the identity of the abbey is lost with the coming of the sixteenth century Reformation. However today both Roman Catholics and Protestants can share the rich history of the foundation, as the ecumenical movement in Ulster undergoes some momentum. The Anglo-Normans also had their abbots of the monastery, starting with the rule of Maurice in 1178, to William O'Dorman, ruling from 1542. Three important events run on from O'Dorman's rule; The Down Petition, c.1498 and the dissolution of the Abbey of Bangor in 1542. The history of the abbey from its foundation in AD 558 to its dissolution in 1542, is entirely Catholic, with a strong emphasis upon the Roman connection. Today the abbey looks out across the waters of Belfast Lough to the skyline of County Antrim that has not changed much since the sixth century.

Chapter 5

The Concept of Kingship

The concept of kingship goes back far into the history of Ulster and the rest of Ireland and is part of the rich legacy of the past. It is not quite clear if the Ard Rí or king in Ireland was a sacred person. Certainly Jewish kingship in the Bible was not regarded as divine. Sometimes Christ is portrayed as the Sun god in profane literature. All the tribes have had their kings and their gods, the Jewish and Christian God being monotheistic. The Jewish god was the only one and true god but other civilizations have also insisted that their god was the one and only god. Comgall had studied the history of Israel; he was a very intelligent person and he eventually believed in the primacy of Christ. This he taught the Gaels in the tradition of Saint Patrick. Christ, so Comgall understood, had declared himself to be the son of God. He was mocked on the cross as King of the Jews. A crown of thorns was placed upon his head. He cried out to his God, the God of David, the God of the Jews. God did not eventually desert Christ, who had a glorious resurrection. It was most important to believe in Christ, who reaped plentiful harvests, who assured victory in war and who looked over the cattle, sheep and other animals. He saw to it that there was an abundance of milk, and that the seas and rivers were full of fish.

As in the Bible the reign of an unjust king was condemned. It was up to the people to declare a king as being evil and unjust, for an unjust king brought war, famine and scarcity in his train. Once elected the king was inaugurated. In the Bible God was consulted with the inauguration of a king. He was the God of Israel, and he had brought Moses and his people out of the land of Egypt, "out of the house of bondage". God had delivered commandments unto Moses, and in Ulster the king was also bound by the Brehon and Gaelic laws. In theory the king was to bring prosperity to his people, and monasticism like that of Bangor was bound to support the autocratic rule of the rí or king.

c

Christ had said that it was important to render "under Caesar the things that are Caesar's, and unto God the things that are God's". In ancient society the king, in some states, was divine. The emperor of Rome was said to be divine, and this led to a conflict between first century Christians at Rome and the imperial authorities. The feast of Tara, when the King of the Uí Neill was solemnly wedded to the goddess of Tara, survived well into Christian times. The druids and law makers dictated their wishes and desires and the king was to be respected. The High-King was a conservative figure, and guardian of the Brehon laws. It was declared that battles were won as a result of the belief in the superstitions of the local kings and the "central" High-Kings. Battles were won as a result of the belief in a deity. This is also common to Comgall Christianity, where the dictum of turning the other cheek was overlooked. Comgall's God was both a God of peace and a God of war, and much of the monasteries must have been based upon the teaching of the Old Testament, an "eye for an eye, a tooth for a tooth, an arm for an arm and a leg for a leg".

For Comgall, man was basically a sinful creature, who had acquired original sin at the time of the Creation. Comgall was well aware that it was important to remain celibate in order to acquire a personal relationship with God. One writer said that "the fruits and plants of the earth have been devastated so that there is neither force in them today to support anyone. The falsehood and sin and injustice of men have robbed the earth of its fruits and their strength and force".

It was important that the king should be a rightful king, for if he was not evil might befall the "state". The image of the pagan king as being potentially evil is perhaps exaggerated, for the rí had to some degree the welfare of his subjects in mind.

The God of the Jews and the God of Comgall therefore had much in common. God understood the failings of the pagans, and declared that he was above the pagan gods of the Romans and the Gaels. It was important to believe the doctrines and dogmas of Comgall's time, for if one did not, then even a righteous man might be cast into Hell. Comgall wished to introduce into Ulster the ceremony of ordaining kings, in line with the practise of other European lands. This would insure the king's Christian character.

Little information has come down to us about the inauguration of kings. The O'Neills of Tyrone were inaugurated on a sacred stone, and a silver slipper was tossed over the king's head. In the Bible kings are ordained as a result of the will of God. In Christian times, the Pope had the power to ordain and also to depose. Republican principles appear to be unheard of in biblical times and in Comgall's monastic sphere he exhorted the Gaels to obey their king — perhaps only if that king believed in God and looked to the leadership of the Catholic primate of Ulster in the island. Inauguration of the Gaelic kings however remained a sacred ceremony, and this has been witness to pagan origins. The idea that Ireland was a person, a beautiful woman who could be sought and won by the rightful king, has survived in Ireland until modern times. In the Bible God is portrayed as a man. He created man in his own image, and it was essential to believe in the father figure of God. God claimed rule over all the earth, which he had created along with the heavens.

Comgall read the opening chapters of Genesis and believed quite literally the story of the six days of Creation, and how God rested from his work on the seventh day, which he hallowed. In pagan literature the Sun god was worshipped on a Sunday. The Christian God eventually became a complex being for he was to rule over national states and empires by the mid twentieth century. The origins for the inauguration of a king is lost to history, for no detailed account has been handed down in the various books and annals. The medieval historian Geraldus Cambrensis has record of a ceremony amongst the Cenel Conaill of Ulster, which is based upon other customs. A white mare is sacrificed, and this represented a territorial god exclusive to the Cenel Conaill. The rí underwent a union with the mare, and he drank of the mare's blood. However it is thought that this practice did not take place later than the twelfth century. It may be that the ceremony of inauguration lasted beyond the sixth century, but for Comgall it was necessary to Christianize the rís and to establish a Christian means of inauguration. In Europe this took the form of the crowning of the king, who held his power by divine right and from the Pope. The pagan ceremony at Bangor took place on a mound, and present were many dignitaries — the poets, the bards, magicians (druids) and other important people in the king's realm or tribal region.

A white rod was generally a symbol of authority. The whiteness of the rod symbolized the righteousness of the king. A poet recited the king's genealogy and sang his praises before the abbey in the Dal Fitach kingdom that embraced North Down. Various other matters of state were recited and these Gaelic customs may have come with the Milesians or Gaels from a base in France or Gaul. At a later date there were medieval poems, which presumably reflected the powers of the church. Advice was given to a new king. There were texts of advice, the most well known of which is the "Audacht Morasud", which however shows no Christian influence.

There is also the "Book of Leinster", which records other details about the workings of a small Gaelic kingdom. Keating, writing in the seventeenth century, states that the dynastic historian or ollam read aloud the principles of kingship at the inauguration, and drew attention to the prosperity that would result from the rule of a righteous king, apart from the reign of Christian kings in Comgall's age.

Basically the ceremony of inauguration was the meeting place of all the great nobles of North Down, as well as members of the clergy by the sixth century. Another institution associated with inauguration was the crech ríg or royal family, by which the rí demonstrated his suitability for office. He acquired great herds of cattle. In early Irish society it was the family and not the individual that held power. Comgall had to preach to the family who accepted the Christian God. The rí followed suit, but this did not guarantee the conversion of the tribe. The joint family was the derbfine and comprised the descendants in the male line of a common great-grandfather. It extended then to the second cousins and not beyond. Comgall laid great emphasis upon the role of the family in the Catholic Church in Ulster. It was a system that may have been borrowed from the European kings.

The European monarchs had borrowed much from the defunct Roman Empire. Comgall's Church was also based at Rome and presumably he was in favour of the European system of monarchy. Monarchy was a divine institution ordained by God in the Old and New Testaments. However the people were remote from the king and it was often the aristocracy that were executed in disputes. It was the dream of the Italian and German princes to recreate the ancient Roman system that had governed Western and Eastern Europe for one thousand years, before its final collapse to Islam in 1453. Comgall of course looked East to Constantinople with its struggles with the Moslems. In his age it was quite a possibility that the Moslems might invade Europe and reach Ulster. Comgall feared that the Church might fall under the rule of the Moslems, bringing all the efforts at Bangor Abbey to nothing. However history was to take a different course. The Turks were content to govern Eastern Europe and to leave the disorganized West European monarchies to themselves. For Comgall the Turk was one of the Antichrists talked about in the Bible. The nations of the West had for some time sent knights to combat the Moslems.

As a great evangelist, Comgall preached the second coming of the Lord, who would judge persons and nations. To enter Heaven the rí had to do good and to have performed good works. Outside of Comgall's Bangor Abbey lay the pagan and the fornicator and to all those who broke the Ten Commandments. Comgall, as a fundamentalist, preached the word of God and the miracles of the Church, more powerful than the miracles and feats of the druid magicians of the remaining pagan kings in Ulster.

Bangor Abbey symbolized the sixth century struggle in Europe for freedom and for some kind of political union. The Papacy urged a return to the Christian values of the fourth century, when the popes blessed the works of the Roman emperors and kings under them. Comgall had a sophisticated view of the Gaelic kings. This unity in Eirinn might take the shape of a reformed High-Kingship and a kingship that was based upon a more centralist theory. The Ard Rí or High-King of course would reflect Christian beliefs. In Europe the sixth century had seen the breakdown of civilization after the collapse of the Roman Empire in the mid fifth century and the flight of the emperors to East Rome at Constantinople. However Comgall wished Bangor Abbey to remain remote from the European kings, but he of course embraced spiritual Rome.

Bangor was one of the many foundations in the Papal system. Comgall received his commission directly from the Pope, and he worked for and only for the Pope or father in Rome, the Vicar of Christ, the Pontifex Maximus and Supreme Pontiff. In early Irish society the family was therefore the legal unit and not the individual. The joint family was the derbfine of "certain kindred" and comprised the descendants in the male line of a common great-grandfather. It was extended then to second cousins and not beyond. These ideas have been made as the result of studies made in the annals, genealogies and law tracts. The idea has been put forward that any member of the royal dynasty, who was with the derbfine of a precious king, was eligible to succeed as rí or king. They bore the title "rigdamna" or "makings of kings", a term which implied this and nothing more. The succession of the Bangor kings was made by election. The law of royal succession, then, was the same as the ordinary law of succession to property. Under the Anglo-Saxon system the eldest son succeeded to the property of his father. This may have had its origins dating back to the succession of kings in the Bible.

The Anglo-Saxons had for some time their eyes upon Ireland, but it was not until the twelfth century under the Norman monarchy, that the English kings assumed control of Ireland, proclaiming themselves as "lords" of the country. Comgall no doubt was able to appreciate the Anglo-Saxon system in the sixth century, but he basically supported the Gaelic law in relation to the concept of kingship. Comgall was aware that the monastery of Bangor had a very special place in the Gaelic law, for as abbot Comgall was called upon to support the political status quo in Ulster. The rí attended mass at the abbey at regular intervals, accepting the system of the Catholic Church. The druids had their place in the Gaelic law, for their support of the pagan kingship was important for the credibility of a ruler. The druids had been discredited by Saint Patrick, so Comgall's task was to carry on good relations with the newly converted kings. For Comgall the individual believer was important for the success of the Church, both at Rome, and by Comgall's successors. The Bible was also a book that spoke to both the individual in the Church and to the assemblies within it.

Catholicism embraced many ideas and heresies, but the Roman Church had survived by the time of Comgall's foundation at Bangor in AD 558. However, the Church, to Comgall, may have been Italian in origin, for it was in the Italian peninsula and in its states, that the Pope claimed to rule over. Had Christ given Peter a political commission as well? Peter was a man, with all the weaknesses of the individual. His faith could waver, the Church might make erroneous statements, but the general consensus was that the Pope was infallible when he talked on matters of faith and doctrine. Peter had symbolically been given the keys of the kingdom of Heaven; whatever God willed the Church would carry out, and whatever Peter said would be supported by his maker. The Papacy was to be an elective monarchy, the college of cardinals elected a Pope, but there was no reference to cardinals in the Bible or in the primitive Church. The Gaelic laws recognized the episcopal system, or rule by the bishops, over the Church. The first popes were called Bishops of Rome, and in comparison to other sees, the city of Rome was quite new. The Gaelic laws recognized the need for order in society, despite the diversity caused by the confederate nature of the High-Kings. The kings acknowledged Comgall's Bishop of Rome as being a superior kind of king than the Irish tribal rís. By the sixth century episcopal law had been established in Eirinn, and it underlined the need for obedience to the kings. This was a process that could be dated back to the time of Saint Patrick, who reformed the Brehon or Gaelic laws in favour of the Church. The sixth century kings were both loyal to the Church and to what was left of paganism, a process that had been afoot in the Roman Empire of the fourth century.

The Gaelic kings "ran with horses and hunted with the hounds". However Comgall was a dedicated man, and believed like Patrick, that the Church should have absolute power over the kings and their subjects.

The abbey looked over a kingship that was not normally divisible. The institution of tanaise or heir designate, the naming of a successor in the king's lifetime, had been fully developed by the sixth century. The office of tanaise is a very ancient Irish institution, the word "tanaise" meaning "the expected one". Irish dynasties, much to Comgall's disapproval, were polygamous from the early period to the final eclipse of paganism. This meant that there were large numbers of claimants to the Irish tuatha "thrones". In actual fact it was the strongest members of the dynasty that succeeded. Succession was determined by family power politics. The strongest succeeded, the weakest went to the wall. Each dynasty was constantly divided amongst itself, and Comgall quoted the gospels, that a house divided against itself could not rule, but would perish.

It may be that Comgall wanted to bring the Gaelic tuatha into political conformity within the concept of kingship in Europe. This meant that there were constant struggles in society for the price of the kingship. Sixth century Ulster was a society in which there were too many leaders of the opposition, far more than the segregated nature of Ulster politics today. Division seems to have been the rule during most ages in Ulster's politics and history, but Comgall's Church had come to bring spiritual aid to Ulaid or Ulster in an age of political disintegration.

Chapter 6

The Bangor Antiphonary

The manuscript known as the Bangor Antiphonary is said to date back to the seventh century, but it could have been penned by the great Comgall himself. It ranks as one of the great religious works of Western Civilization. There are many other books recounting the political and religious life of the Ulster clans and the Irish people. To start with there is the great "Confession" of Saint Patrick, a work of piety, written in Latin. Other manuscripts accumulated through the course of time were kept in the monasteries by the great professors of Irish literature.

The creed found in the Bangor work differs from all others known and is in substance the original creed of Nicea, meeting in AD 325 at Nicea (now Iznik) in Turkey. Comgall's world could look back to the second century of the Christian Church by which time the Church had developed a clear system of authority based mainly on the Scriptures, its creed and its hierarchy of bishops, priests and deacons. This early Christianity is reflected in the Bangor Antiphonary. Comgall participated fully in the life of the Church. He strove to understand the mass, the sacraments, and the role of the Virgin Mary in the economy of salvation. The Bangor Antiphonary starts "In the name of God". It starts with the song of Moses. The book itself does not provide us with any inkling of who it was written by. It says that the heavens should listen "to what I have to say". The earth should hear the word of the author of the Antiphonary.

The opening is "Protestant" and evangelical, it is not concerned overtly with doctrine and dogma. It is written in biblical language and has all the authority of Scripture. Back to these books the Church fathers return in their quest to carry out the commands of the first Christians. The Antiphonary claims that its words are like rain and it says that the ordinary Gael would be inspired by its teaching. This falls into line with the other great works of piety that the Church produced from the time of Christ to Comgall's Bangor in the sixth century.

It says that one has to call upon the word of the Lord, but it makes no mention of the Virgin Mary and the modern Papal claims. It says that it calls upon the word of the Lord, making claim that there was an infallible Bible as well as an infallible Pope guarding the Church.

The monks poured over their manuscripts in the monastery, and Bangor Abbey must have produced quite a number of these books. These works of God are perfect and are a model for living. It claimed that "Those who have sinned are not like children in their evil". Like the Bible it claims that the present generation has fallen from grace. Comgall believed that man was basically a wicked creature; he had fallen from grace in the Garden of Eden. Christ had come to save the Roman Empire from Hell, and the Church was to be established at Rome. Christ, of course, though a man, was free from original sin, along with his mother, the Virgin Mary. The Antiphonary acknowledges and endorses the life of Christ and the importance of the crucifixion and resurrection of the Lord.

The generations of Gaels did not know how to repay the Lord for all his goodness. The purpose of the Antiphonary is to assert the divinity and saving nature of Christ, the purpose of all the great fathers and documents of the Church. It says: "Is this the way you repay the Lord, O foolish and stupid people. Is he not your father, to whom you belong and who made you and created you". Emphasis is laid upon the previous generation of Christians, how they were very close to Christ and his mother. The Gaels are exhorted to remember the previous generations. One had to ask the Lord and he will tell you. Above all else the average Gael had to listen, hear and recognize the word of the Lord.

The Antiphonary was perhaps produced as a teaching work, but we gain no inkling of the character of Comgall from it, or indeed if he was the author. The manuscripts and books were produced mainly by anonymous authors, and great books like that of the Book of Kells remain without an author (The Book of Kells may have been penned by Saint Columba, at a slightly later date than Comgall's works). The Antiphonary states that God divided the people of the earth, at the time of the Tower of Babel, and he confused the tongues of the people, forming them into nations with different languages. The Gaels of course had their own language, which was perhaps derived from the Near East, although it reached maturity in the years of the European Celts, or the Celtic "Empire". God established the frontiers of the nations, and the frontiers of Rome had also been set by God. The Christian, both in Ireland and in the Empire, had little time for the Romans; Britain had been conquered by the Empire, and Ireland always lived in fear of an invasion. The Antiphonary speaks to the religion of the Gaels, claiming that God would look after Ulster.

Christianity was basically a religion of the great cities of the Roman Empire. Such cities did not exist in Ireland on a European scale. In Ulster the nearest thing to a city was Emain Macha or Armagh, which became the Primatial See at the time of Saint Patrick. The Antiphonary shows no sign of pagan influence; the atmosphere is Old Testament and the language that of the Latin evangelist. These books no doubt copied the language of the Bible. There were also the works of the Latin and Greek Church fathers that were written in a highly evangelical note. Comgall himself was both monk and evangelist, but before all else he trusted in the saving word of the Bible.

In the sixth century, with the overthrow of civilization in Europe, it was essential "to hold fast that which was good". It is not known how many manuscripts there were like the Bangor Antiphonary that were penned in Ulster and the other Irish kingdoms. Probably the number runs into thousands, but few of them have come down to us. These books tell how God created man and woman higher than the beasts of the fields. "He placed him high upon the earth, to eat the fruits of the fields and to suck honey from the rock and olive oil from the hardest stone". However the history of Israel is a history of a nation falling away from God, as is the history of every other nation, the Irish not excluded. The Papacy was a worldly organization, and it would reflect human weakness, for had not the popes developed sophisticated doctrines that many believe are not based upon either the Bible or tradition or the teachings of the Church councils and synods. The Ulster Gaels had no representation at the early Church councils, so they relied upon Rome and the Pope to guide them in Christian matters.

Today there is no other greater Papal country than Ireland, and Comgall is highly praised in the history of the Irish nation. Bangor Abbey, although there are no remains, is a great treasure for the Catholic world. The monks exhorted in their great book that the faithful should "drink the pure juice of the grape". In the Antiphonary there is a celebration of Bangor's contribution to Church history; "The Holy valiant deeds / of the sacred Fathers, / Based on the great / Church of Bangor; / The noble deeds of abbots, / Their number, times and names / Of never ending lustre, / Hear brothers; great their deserts, / What the Lord hath gathered / To the mansions of the heavenly kingdom / Christ loved Comgall, / Well, too, did he the Lord".

Saint Comgall's feast day is the 10th May, and he has been called "the light of the world". As he read the Antiphonary he could look back to his schooling under Saint Finnian at Clonenagh in County Laois, later going to Glasnevin where he met Saint Columba or Columcille and Saint Ciaran of Clonmacnoise. Upon his return to Ulster he founded the Bangor monastery in AD 558. For youth Comgall was an authority figure, and he believed that this authority was gradually developed over many centuries by the Catholic Church. This attitude is entirely biblical and Comgall must have looked up to Saint Paul as one of the great saints of the "ecclesia". The Bible had authority, for in it, for saints and sinners, was the word of God. However there was also the Apocryha or deutero-canonical books which the Roman Church received and the Protestant Churches later rejected. Saint Paul says in his epistle to the Corinthians "God has given the first place to the apostles, the second to the prophets, the third to the teachers; after them miracles, and after that the gift of healing; helpers, good leaders, those with many languages". For Comgall, like Saint Paul, the apostleship was not only confined to the direct followers of Christ, but to all the prophets and saints of the Church, outside of the original twelve.

Comgall's rule is said to have been very strict; he probably looked up to Saint Paul and his rigorous lifestyle. Comgall at first ate only one meal a day, but when his health started to suffer, he reviewed his diet. Wonderful gardens have often been the centre of great monasteries and convents, and Bangor, with its abundance of fruit, vegetables, herbs and flowers was no exception. At one stage Comgall discovered thieves stealing from his monastery, and he prayed that they should be forgiven. He hated all kinds of criminals. The next time that the thieves stole from the garden they were blinded. They stumbled around and sought forgiveness of Comgall, who forgave them, their sight being restored.

On one occasion the monastery was short of grain. As a great artist and humanitarian, Comgall recited his prayers to God to bring good fortune to the farmers. The monastery's leaders looked forward to a visit from Saint Columba to Bangor Abbey. Comgall prayed for a continuous supply of food. There was a great catch of fish in Belfast Lough, and the monks cooked the fish for their guests. The four thousand monks and students at the monastery became known as the "Vale of the saints". Many years later the monastery was described by Saint Bernard of Clonmacnoise as "truly sacred, the nursery of saints". Two of Comgall's monks founded a monastery at Paisley in Scotland. During the Viking raids, Bangor suffered the loss of 900 monks. Some important relics of the abbey come down to us — the Bull of Bangor, preserved in the Bangor heritage centre and the Antiphonary of Bangor, now housed in the Ambrosian Library in Milan.

Comgall was aware that the Gaels had sacrificed and worshipped strange gods. This is made clear in the Antiphonary; "they sacrificed to demons and false gods whom they did not know and not the true God". It also went on to say that the Gaels had tended to abandon their God and that they forgot their Creator. The entire message of Christianity in works like the Antiphonary is the overriding power of God and his ability to punish the sinner. The Christian and the pagan were both capable of sinning, the Christian by turning away from God and the pagan by openly defying the saving power of Christ.

It is not known at what part of Comgall's career that he planned to set up his famous abbey. Missionary work amongst the Ulster tribes must have inspired him, but overall his ambition was to bring the word to the

European mainland. Civilization was in decline with the fall of West Rome in the mid fifth century. He had no idea that as a young man he would become abbot of one of Ulster's greatest monasteries that ranked with Glendalough and Clonmacnoise in the south of Ireland.

The Bangor Antiphonary records that a hymn was sung during holy communion to the priests; "Come forward, you who are holy. Receive the body of Christ and drink the sacred blood by which you will be redeemed". Clearly the Church at Bangor believed in some form of primitive holy communion; like holy communion in the present day Anglican Church and in the Church of Ireland. Holy communion is ranked with the sacraments of the Church, and the churches have differed since the Reformation about how many sacraments there are. The Anglicans point to two sacraments, but the High Church, like the Roman Church, believe in seven sacraments. The primitive Churches believed that it was necessary to drink the blood and eat the flesh of Christ to be admitted to the Catholic Church to assure one's self of salvation. This surely was Comgall's faith, the faith of Patrick, the faith of Columba. The hymn stated that "Christ Himself, the Lord, Alpha and Omega, has come and will come again to judge mankind". There is another hymn, a hymn to Saint Patrick, teacher of the Irish. He is described as a steadfast man, who was never shaken from his faith. Like Saint Peter he is described as a Rock of the Church. Before the gates of Heaven the powers of darkness would perish. God had chosen Comgall to teach the barbarians, as the early Church regarded the Irish, who however had an advanced form of civilization dating back in the island for many centuries.

Like Patrick and Columba, Comgall renounced all worldly goods and ambitions to become a monk and eventually to be the first abbot of Bangor Mor (Bangor the Great). There is also included a hymn to Saint Comgall. From this we learn a little of his character, but the emphasis is upon his piety and ability as an evangelist. The hymn describes the Church as living in an age of decay, either in the sixth or seventh centuries. The Romans were said to be decadent during the final decline in the mid fifth century. Ireland was a very old culture, and was vulnerable to new ideas like the importance of the Church in the fifth and sixth century age. However the ecclesiastical foundations in Ireland did not reflect this decay, nor the churches and monasteries in dark age Europe. Glendalough is one of the best known Celtic pilgrimage sites. Unlike Bangor, there are extensive remains. There is a round tower, churches, lakes and mountains. Glendalough means "the valley of the two lakes". It is likely that Comgall may have visited Glendalough along with his other travels as Abbot of Bangor throughout Eirinn. Like Comgall, Saint Kevin, founder of Glendalough, was born in the sixth century of a noble family. Like Comgall from an early age he was outstanding for certain gifts. Like Comgall he was educated at a variety of institutions until he eventually ran away from the Gaelic establishment, hiding out in the Wicklow mountains. However the monks found him and he was forced back to full time education, until he was eventually ordained as a priest.

As in Bangor, the church at Glendalough produced a variety of books. Unlike Bangor, the Glendalough monastery had only about 1,000 pupils. At Kevin's death in AD 618 the monastery was just coming into its own. Like Bangor, Glendalough was plundered by the Vikings, who sacked the monastery in either the fifth or eighth centuries. The Bangor Antiphonary represents the triumph of civilization over what remained of paganism in the island. It is penned by the hand of an educated man, who had deep Christian beliefs. It is all that has survived the centuries, and the work can be regarded as truly Roman and Catholic. Comgall, as well as being a great evangelist, was above all else a Pope's man, looking to Rome for a simple form of guidance, for Comgall was always aware that God meant his Church to have clear visible foundations in the violent and decadent world of the declining Roman Empire. That other great saint of the period is Saint Ciaran of Clonmacnoise, whose feast day is the 5th March. The monastery was like Bangor dramatically situated next to water, along the broad River Shannon.

Ciaran, the founder of Clonmacnoise, was born in AD 515. The sixth century is an age of great saints in the Irish Church. His father was also born at Larne like Comgall. He was a chariot builder, living in the lands of the Latharna tribe. Like Comgall Ciaran was given the benefit of a good education. He studied at various monasteries, until at length he founded Clonmacnoise in AD 549, a little while before Comgall founded Bangor in AD 558.

Clonmacnoise, like Bangor, had a large number of pupils. Here scribes studied Latin poems, arithmetic, music, astronomy, astrology, mechanics and medicine. The monastery occupied a site of approximately ten acres but the extent of the Bangor monastery — the larger — is unknown. But Ciaran died of a fever seven years after the foundation of Clonmacnoise monastery.

Now back at Bangor, we find Comgall ready to set sail for Scotland with his close friend Molaing, to join Saint Columba on the island of Iona, which was to become perhaps more famous than the Irish foundation. Columba had founded a monastery at Derry (Doire), on a site of land that was given to him by the local rí or king. The voyage from Derry to Iona took a couple of days with a good wind. Now Comgall and Molaing, probably with other saints, set sail from the coast of Down. Comgall realized that he was sailing into danger for the Picts of Scotland were notorious for their cruelty and their dislike of Christianity. Comgall always had in mind throughout the expedition the great book Bangor Abbey had produced for civilization.

Chapter 7

The Nature of Society

Ulster society in the sixth century was intensively aristocratic and also very hierarchical, a society that in the ancient law tracts that was divided into three grades — kings, lords and commons. This is also a position reflected in other European societies of the age, when the king played the key role, under him being the nobles and commoners. All the major world religious systems have had their hierarchical systems. The Jews in Palestine had theirs, and the emphasis has been on a Messiah that will come to save the nations. The coming of Christ, so Comgall understood, was well documented in the Bible, but the Jews rejected the Messiah in the beginning of the first century, for they demanded that Christ should be put to death.

History depicts Christ being put to death on a cross, but some authorities think it was a simple stake. The Jews of the period relied heavily on traditions, traditions which Christ condemned. He said that the Jews perverted the word of God by their traditions. Comgall was of course aware that the Church relied heavily upon tradition, a position that Lutheranism and Anglicanism take up when criticizing the Roman Catholic Church. Both Protestants and Roman Catholics, since the Reformation, have agreed that there should be some sort of authority in society that would guide the Church and the nation states.

The Church blessed the system of kingship, for the Irish kings and High-Kings, and Comgall remembered the dictate of Christ — "render unto Caesar the things which are Caesar's and unto God the things that are God's". In Ulster the classes moved amongst each other, rather like modern Northern Ireland, and societies elsewhere in the West. All were united in some sort of obedience to the rí and to the Ard Rí or High-King, but Comgall never expected that there might be some sort of confederate system in Ireland, something greater than the Ard Rí ship of the sixth century. Comgall looked across Europe to the many political systems, all looking to Rome for spiritual and political inspiration. He may have envisaged another Roman Empire, or the expansion of East Rome back into Europe, to Britain and indeed to Ulster. In the age of Comgall the Roman system in the West had only fallen 150 years before. There was the position of the Church that Comgall believed that might bring about some kind of unity in Europe. Europe was to wait until the ninth century for some kind of unity in the West to take place under the Holy Roman Empire and the emperor Charlemagne, who again may have looked westwards to Britain and Ireland/Ulster.

The Gaels minded their own business but by the age of Charlemagne the migration of people into the Empire, had reached its peak. The Gaels of Magheramourne and Bangor were proud of their green land, and expected that their abbot Comgall would support all their efforts at unity. The sixth century Gaels must have envisaged some sort of unity for the island. The kings of the Ulaid had sometimes, along with the Uí Neill, asserted their position in Eirinn. Comgall himself, like the great notables in Irish history, may have been related to a royal house. Perhaps he envisaged an Ireland rather like that of the Holy Roman Empire. Certainly the Italians, French and Spanish of the period had great respect for the Irish, and could not understand why they could not create more unity.

In Ulster the noble was distinguished from the commoner; apart from birth and wealth he was in possession of clients, men bound to him by specific degrees of dependence. The commons or grád Fhéne were freeholders with full legal rights, and the general name for them was "aithech", which meant "rent-payer". Again this system is reflected in the later Empire, and it is highly likely that the Irish commoner had rights similar to other European societies that they may have sprang from. The Gaelic commoners' representative was the bó-aire, usually independent farmers, in many ways similar to the Anglo-Saxon churl. Comgall is likely to have endorsed the status quo in Ulster, but he was a rebel as far as matters of faith and belief were concerned.

All the great European states appear to have had their own religious champions, who have endorsed the existing religious system. As in Europe the Pope was above the many monarchs, who held their thrones from the Papacy. The High-King held his throne by rite of being the largest cattle owner in Ireland. Kingdoms like that of North Down had a limited number of cattle, together with other livestock. Beneath the commoners on the social and economic scale were the bothach or "cottier" and they differed very little from the nothach. These commoners held their land from a lord in return for services. The fuidir was also equally bound by uncertain services, and seems to have been a tenant settled by a lord on his superfluous land. These commoners could very quickly descend to the level of an sen-cheithe, an hereditary serf bound to the soil, and was part and parcel of his lord's estate. On the basis of class distinction the Brehon lawyers defined and carried out the Gaelic laws. The Brehons date back to the coming of the Gaels or Milesians to Ireland, many centuries before the birth of Christ. The law they brought to Ulster had a European origin, for we have seen that the Gaels or Celts may have come from a base in the Alps or from Spain, sailing across the Spanish Sea to the ports of southern and eastern Ireland. The Celts are recorded in Caesar's Gallic wars, and Caesar says that the Celts of Gaul were driven back by the Roman legions, across the English Channel and into Britain. In turn the Celts of Britain again under Roman pressures, in the first century, were driven west across Britain, where they sailed across the Irish Sea into the ports of eastern Ireland.

Caesar recorded quite a developed Celtic civilization. There was, to some extent, a Celtic Empire that could unite Ireland and hold together the lands of the former Roman Empire. The Gaelic laws were in Ulster and the other provinces committed to memory. But these laws may have been written down with the advent of Saint Patrick, who reformed the Brehon laws. The Brehons were also judges and sat in the Gaelic courts. All societies have had their social systems, usually based upon political beliefs. We do not know what Comgall's political persuasion was, whether he was a liberal or a conservative. Suffice to say that he was a believer in the Latin and Greek Church. Comgall urged his fellow Christians to obey the Gaelic laws, but this was easier said than done now that the laws had been reformed.

The socio-economic aspect of the system was the institution of clientship or célsine by which dependant relatives were established amongst the men. There were two main classes of clientship, sóer-rath and gíallnae. The former may be translated as free fief, and may be understood to mean free of noble clientship. A man received a fief of stock from a lord, and paid back the money at an annual rate of interest of thirty-three and a third per cent over seven years. At the end of the seven years the capital advanced became his absolute property and the contract was terminated unless a new fief was accepted by the client. The client was usually a freeholder and in free clientship with the noble, who maintained his independent status but was due to pay homage to his lord. In return the lord was called upon to defend his client's rights.

The Bible however condemned usury and Christ spoke out about it, although Comgall probably endorsed systems of moderate loans. In the medieval Italy of the popes usury was big business and the Catholic Church supported the economic policies of the many leaders of Rome, Florence and Venice. This was the age of great colour and of materialistic Christianity. The colourful nature of Ulster society can be dated back to the sixth century to men like Comgall who were devout Pope's men. Perhaps loans were not important for the vast majority of people in the sixth century. They were too poor to take out a loan, and these loans were the prerogative of the upper classes and the various tribal leaders, chiefs,

47

lords and kings. The Church itself regarded money as a useful commodity in sixth century Ulster. Money could make a poor man's life happier and no doubt the many kings in Ulster endorsed the money lending policies of the Catholic Church, and other great institutions in society. The Bible's attitude to wealth and its flaunting is quite clear, for Christ had said that the poor would enter the kingdom of Heaven, and that it was easier for a camel to pass through the eye of a needle than for a rich man to enter the kingdom of God.

Ulster society in the sixth century was much less nationalistic than the kingdoms of divided Europe. In Europe tribalism had been completely left behind and by the ninth century Charlemagne had been in power at his capital Aachan for a number of years. However even though Irish society was fragmented, this did not prevent the age of art and learning flourishing at monasteries like that of Bangor. In Europe the money system had been highly developed as in modern society, whilst in Ulster emphasis was laid upon evangelicalism and the wisdom that the priests and monks shared with the people. There was also the system of gíallnae, based upon clientship. The lord advanced to his client a fief of stock and other goods in return for which the client paid his lord interest of one unit in twelve per annum at eight and a half per cent or its equivalent. The tenant paid a considerable food-rent, and rendered fixed labour services. The lord granted him an initial payment equal to his status in the tuatha. The relationship between lord and base client could be terminated at will. However the Gaelic laws were slanted towards the lord and not the base client. In modern society we live in an economy that is geared towards people borrowing money at a rate of interest. This reflects a highly developed economy in the West, greater than the economic system of Rome and Constantinople. Ulster society can be likened to that of the Greeks whose civilization was based upon the city state, for example Athens. Both societies were warlike, more warlike than the Europe of the German emperor Charlemagne.

Comgall must have looked back at the warlike tribes and societies of Old Testament times, when there was exacted "an eye for an eye and a tooth for a tooth" for sinners. Under the Gaelic laws, and the law of Christ, sin was severely punished, but in the pagan system murder was only punished by a heave fine, whereas under the New Testament murder was punished by death. Ulster society has advanced from those days, and murder is now punished by life imprisonment.

There were many wars between the tuatha in Ulster, and it was impractical to catch murderers in the tribal setting. After the sixth century the grades of commons seems to have been increased, due probably to a general increase of the population. Before the beginning of the ninth century and probably much earlier, the derbfine joint-family and property owning kindred group, had fallen into decadence and was replaced by the family which because it was smaller and less able to defend itself, became increasingly dependent upon lordly protection.

Increase in population was also a European phenomenon, for the barbarians had pressed hard upon the frontiers of the Roman Empire, eventually sacking Rome itself stealing the wealth of the Christian emperors and the monasteries. These barbarians, like Rome, left the Gaels of Ireland to lead their own lives. The sister island of Britain also fell under barbarian attack, with the coming of the Anglo-Saxons, who eventually embraced Christianity. The Ulster of Comgall was perhaps only 500,000, whilst modern Ulster boasts 1,500,000, about a third of these being Roman Catholics. With a small population it was easier to carry out the task of evangelization, whereas in Europe, conversions may have taken place slowly as the Church in Italy, France and Spain, wanted a permanent end of paganism.

In sixth century Ulster there were polygamous marriages, resulting in an increase of the population. Chiefs and lords easily slipped down the social ladder, causing disruption in society. In mainland Britain this was a situation that obtained also, where the lords and barons lost their lands and sank to the level of the commoners. The average lordly Gael of Comgall's North Down would not have liked their change in status, and perhaps the tendency was to steal cattle and livestock of successful lords in order to support themselves. The ruined aristocracy took to the hills and other higher places, raiding traders on their way from major centres in the north of Ireland. In Comgall's day there were a number of highways, the greatest one being the North-South Highway that ran from Tara north of Dublin to Dunseverick at Bebane Head, capital of the kingdom of Dalriada. There was probably a road leading from Emain Macha or Armagh traversing central Ulster, running through the Belfast region to the shores of North Down and Bangor Abbey.

The observance of the rule of law is important to all civilized societies, states and empires. The rule of law at the time of the Roman Empire enabled Saint Paul and the other disciples to travel around the Mediterranean and even further afield. To this extent Saint Comgall was a Roman, in that he supported the more civilized Empire, even though he was living 150 years after its fall.

It is not known when the apostles wrote the gospels. Paul is the most prolific writer, and as we have seen, Peter only wrote a few letters. In comparison with the Old Testament, the New Testament is quite small, judging by the importance of its message. The early Christians were accused of all sorts of crimes and the Jews exhorted the Empire to persecute them: Christians actually believed that God had become man and dwelt amongst the nations of the Holy Land. In Ulster the early Christians were free to follow their beliefs, due perhaps to the small size of the overall population of the island. Comgall's abbey did not challenge the powers

D

that existed, he only wanted the kingdom to follow the new faith, for he believed that God had in fact become man and had been crucified for the sins of all mankind. The Church had its own laws, doctrines and dogmas which were essential for salvation. This was also true of the pagan religions of Ulster that pre-dated the arrival of Christianity.

The druids had taught that there were nature gods along with the god of the Sun. These religions, like the religions of the Old Testament, demanded human sacrifice, but not so in Ulster. Human sacrifice is to be identified with the European and British druids and other pagan cults. The original Gaels or Milesians that had settled in Ulster before the time of Christ were colonizing forces who dominated and killed the original population. This is entirely in keeping with the movements of tribes in the Old Testament, for did not the children of Israel displace other tribes in the land after the departure from Egypt many years before the advent of the Gaels in Ulster. However neither the Gaels or the Jews built an empire. The Jews went their own way, and the Christians theirs.

History shows that the Church was a strong spiritual force in the world if we are to judge by the number of converts as the criterion for belief. Today the religions in Ulster have declined in number since the sixth century, a very Catholic age. Church attendance in the Roman Church worldwide has declined since the feverish days of nineteenth century Catholicism. Much of Christianity both in the sixth century and in the modern age is based upon liberal principles. Many have declared that they believe in a symbolic Christ, who did not undergo resurrection, and that the Virgin Mary could not have given birth to Christ without having had sexual intercourse with Joseph.

Comgall insisted that only a priest could interpret the Bible for its followers, and that it was important to carry out the dictates of the Church fathers, the most recent in Ulster being Saint Patrick. However the Roman Catholic Church under Pope John Paul II, has agreed that a knowledge of the Bible is useful for the average Christian, and that Anglicans and other communions, are separated brethren. It is doubtful if Comgall was alive today that he would have been a Roman Catholic. His faith would perhaps have agreed with the beliefs of the Anglican Church, i.e., its English variety or the present day Church of Ireland, a "low" Anglican Church. Comgall was a great leader of the Church. Along with Saint Patrick, Columba and Saint Brigid. He cared for all interests in sixth century Ulster and Ireland and he saw the coming and going of many kings in Ulster and many kings on the Continent. He was a Gael, but he did not believe in the concept of an Irish "nation" or an "empire" under the High-Kings. As we shall see, Comgall may have laboured under the Viking threat, for some authorities believe that the Norse were active in Ulster/Ireland from as early as the fourth century. They may have come as simple farmers, making treaties with the rís or kings.

The Celtic round tower (Bangor must have had one) therefore may date back to earlier centuries, for the Gaels are thought to have built round towers in order to hide from the Vikings. They climbed up the tower, taking their gold and silver chalices and crosses with them, but generally they fell under the Viking sword in later incursions of the late eighth and ninth centuries.

Chapter 8

"A Remnant of Chaos"

Egypt has its pyramids, but Ulster from the beginning of time has had its Giant's Causeway, a great miracle to the people of sixth century Ulster, and a phenomenon that the High-Kings could be proud of. It is likely that the early monks of the Gaelic Church took themselves to the tranquillity of the Causeway in order to get closer to Christ. The pagans may also have done this, but no one until recent times could explain the existence of the Giant's Causeway. The gods had been at work on the North Antrim coast and the pagans no doubt may have had an explanation about its origin. An explanation is left to the development of the sciences of geography and geology. The Gaels of North Down, under Comgall, would travel north over the Antrim Plateau to this marvellous rock formation. Alternatively Comgall would sail past the little port of Larne, up the dramatic scenery of the Antrim coast until at length he reached the Giant's Causeway and Coleraine (Cul Rath Ean) area. The journey by currach or skin covered boat would have taken about twenty-four hours, the journey inland by chariot or cart would have been slightly longer. The whole of pagan Ireland had heard about the Causeway and its legendary creator, Finn Mac Coul. Other basaltic formations have been found elsewhere in the world, and have been named after giants or other supernatural forces. There is a Pavé des Géants in France, the Devil's Restplace in California, and Pooningbah, an Australian aboriginal site, in New South Wales, also known as the Giant's Causeway, but in this case associated with a legendary giant.

The Antrim Causeway as far as it is known is listed in the Ulster annals. We are left to conjecture what formed the causeway before the advent of modern science. In ancient Gaelic Ulster giants and ogres roamed the land. Giants are also known in the Bible (Goliath) and are generally portrayed as wicked creatures. How tall these giants were is a matter of conjecture. Finn Mac Coul of the Causeway is portrayed as a formidable giant. The Causeway is continued in Staffa off the south west Scottish coast, discovered by Sir Joseph Banks, explorer and naturalist; he publicized the phenomenon. The rocks emerged from the sea at Fingal's Cave and in very ancient times there may have been a land bridge between Ulster and the west of Scotland.

The Causeway guides tell us that there are various explanations for the rock formations. The Rev William Hamilton, an eighteenth century naturalist and author, records his view of the Causeway: "The native inhabitants of the coast, as they were the earliest observers of this wonder, so they were first to account for its production, and however rude and simple their theory may be, yet a little consideration will satisfy us, that it does not deserve the ignominious appellation of being grossly barbarous and absurd". Another writer in 1793, also described the Causeway and said that the accounts of the creation of the Causeway were a bit far fetched.

It is the story of Finn Mac Coul that however has survived. The site of the Causeway for many centuries may have lain deserted before the medieval period. Explanations for the building of the Causeway were left to Comgall's age, which was curious about the geology of Ulster and the rest of Ireland. In ancient times Roman merchants may have reached the shores of North Antrim and Magheramourne, Comgall's birthplace. Is the story of Finn Mac Coul history or fable? His name is immortalized throughout the Celtic fringe of the British Isles. It may be that he was a figure in ancient Gaelic history. The Finnian tales are part of the Ossian cycle of Irish storytelling, describing the activities of Finn along with his band of warriors, the Fianna. Some think that the historical Finn Mac Coul dates back to the third century, when King Cormac mac Airt was ruling. Finn loved to hunt in the Ulster forests and hills with his faithful warriors, and his exploits today make good reading for children and for the scholar of Celtic studies. Finn had roamed the north coast of Ulster in mythological times, where he could look across the narrow sea to Kintyre, and the isles of Scotland. Scotland was the home of his rival Benandonner, who challenged Finn's strength and reputation. As the two giants never met, Finn decided to write to his rival to engage in a decisive fight. However Finn soon realized that Benandonner was of a superior strength than his own capabilities.

Finn had built a highway from the Giant's Causeway to Scotland, to make the passage easier for the Scottish giant. Finn fled upon news of Benandonner, taking refuge with his wife, Onagh. She disguised Finn as a baby and she placed him in a hastily constructed cradle. She advised Finn to pretend to sleep as the shadow of the Scottish Scots giant fell across the door. Onagh invited Benandonner for tea, pleading with him to be silent lest he woke Finn's child. He took one look at the "child" and judging by its size he fled from the scene, for if Finn's child was such a size what would Finn himself be like! Another legend states that Finn engaged in battle with a British giant; Finn was of enormous size and he lifted earth from central Ulster in the Lough Neagh region and flung it into the Irish Sea, creating the Isle of Man and Lough Neagh.

By the middle of the nineteenth century the volcanic origins of the Causeway was widely accepted. Comgall would perhaps disagree with the explanation for it went against the Creation story in the Book of Genesis. To understand the origin of the Giant's Causeway it is useful to understand the geology. Physical forces were in force for a period of 600 million years, but in geological terms this is quite recent, for the accepted age of the earth is estimated as 4.5 billion years. One must understand the theory of the "big bang" to understand the origins of the Giant's Causeway.

Perhaps the Universe was formed in a day. In Genesis we have learnt that God created the heavens and the earth in six days (what is a day but the flight of a bird through a room) when one takes into account the vast powers of the Creator, the Jewish and Christian God.

For Comgall the Giant's Causeway was an outward manifestation of the unlimited power of Christ. The origin of the Giant's Causeway ranks with the story of Moses's flight from Egypt, with the dividing of the waters of the Red Sea, so that the children of Israel might escape Pharaoh.

On a clear day at the Causeway it is possible to see the Inishowen peninsula of Donegal in the west. The story of the Giant's Causeway can be dated back to prehistoric times. In the Bible there is little reference to large animals — none have been recorded as entering Noah's Ark. Presumably in the rain forests and valleys remains of these animals have yet to be found.

Judaism is an entirely "new" and "recent" religion, along with Christianity. Earthquakes in the very early stages of Judaism are not recorded in the Bible. The Antrim Plateau is volcanic, and some mountains like that of Slemish in mid Antrim dominate the skyline. Comgall would have travelled to Slemish, perhaps on pilgrimage, for at Slemish the great Saint Patrick was enslaved for six or seven years. In the Bible man is the first living creature, not giant animals. The sixth century Church of Comgall however was not aware of modern science, so that the saint believed that God truly created the earth. There were great movements in the earth's crust as the Atlantic Ocean took shape, and the continents of Europe and the Americas were becoming further separated. There followed an intense period of volcanic activity in the North Atlantic, creating large areas of basalt as the outflowing of lava cooled to solid rock. There was also intense volcanic activity in north east Antrim and the west of Scotland. These scenes have not altered since Comgall's day and he must have taken a currach from Larne to visit Scotland, perhaps to the Mull of Kintyre that is visible today from the Antrim coast. He did not go in the fear of a Roman invasion of Ireland, despite the fact that Roman generals had looked out across the Sea of Moyle or North Channel with a view to conquering the country. As we have seen in an earlier chapter, the Romans may have attempted several attempts at invasion, which were however only half hearted. The little port of Larne, dating back to Stone Age times, was a convenient stepping stone for travellers and merchants going to the Western Isles of Scotland and to visit Galloway, which has had a long history of monasticism. Comgall would have visited the "White House" monastery bringing copies of the gospels as presents. The men of Galloway of course marvelled at the achievements of Comgall's Bangor. They too had heard about, and no doubt had visited, the Giant's Causeway which has been called "A remnant of chaos".

The Western Isles and Galloway were all part of the wider Celtic Churches, and they too looked at Rome for guidance if not for absolute authority. Unlike Comgall's Antrim Galloway was relatively a flat piece of land. As the lava poured out at the Giant's Causeway successive layers were created, marked by bands of red laterite (from the Latin word "later", a brick). There were also periods when there was no volcanic activity, the upper parts of the solidified lava weathered under the influence of tropical and dry seasons, forming the red, brown, purple and greyish bands which made up the inter-basaltic beds. Metal obtained in these rocks (mainly iron and basalt), and occasional strips of lignite (decayed plant life also known as brown coal) can still be seen.

For Comgall recorded history may have started in pre-Gaelic times. The saint would have been aware of the various cultures and tribes that made up sixth century Ulster and Ireland. He may have heard of the Tuatha da Danann, who inhabited the Enniskillen region. There were also the pre-Gaelic tribes of the Bangor region, having their origin perhaps in the tribes that inhabited western Britain. It was a short crossing between Galloway and Larne, and between Larne and the Lake District in north west England. The Causeway guides of a later date drew attention to the "sandwich cake" layering of the rocks, often referred to as "trop" rock. The word "trop" is derived from the Swedish word meaning "stair", a good description of the step-like formation of the Giant's Causeway. Maybe Comgall believed that the Causeway was created by mythological forces, but this was probably contrary to his faith, which stated that God had created the Causeway in one day along with the other creatures in the Book of Genesis. For the pagan the gods had created the Causeway, but it is not known if they achieved this in a single day. All civilizations have had their creation stories, perhaps derived from one single account. The Near East and East have been the cradles of civilization, as well as the Irish efforts in the west of Europe. Single God religions like that of Christianity and Islam are supposed to bring us closer to the Creator, rather than make an image of him in order to try to understand him. Comgall lived in a world that knew only Christianity and the pagan beliefs that it overthrew. Comgall no doubt pictured God as a man, for the Bible says that God created man in his own image. All the gods of antiquity are pictured as men and women having supernatural powers. It was essential to believe in these gods in order to have a form of everlasting life. Under the monotheistic system a good life meant belief in God, and belief in God essential for salvation. Much of Christ's teaching is based on the Old Testament books, and certainly Christ viewed it as essential to believe in the laws laid down in the Old Testament.

The pagans viewed the Giant's Causeway, and they attributed it to the work of the gods. It was a testament to their power as they made their presence felt throughout Ulster. If they had created the Giant's Causeway, the powers of the gods would be unlimited, and druidism would survive at Larne, Magheramourne and at Bangor, and at Iona in Scotland. It was not too late for paganism to assert itself in Ireland and further afield. The spiritual world of the Romans might be resurrected and Christianity discredited. Comgall however believed that the Church would last until the end of time, to the second coming of Christ that might take place in his lifetime. Man was buried in order to be resurrected; but there was also purgatory and Hell. Those souls in purgatory would be purged of their sins, so that they could take up their place in Heaven and enjoy everlasting life. Those people who were consigned to Hell would live in eternal torment and would be denied the love of God.

The ancient world had seven wonders, and in modern times the Giant's Causeway is known as the eighth wonder. Comgall would have been aware of these great feats, but also realized that they were a pagan achievement. The wonders of Ulster, as he travelled round the kingdoms, were many. There was Emain Macha or Armagh, (the Primatial See), the North-South Highway from Tara to Dunseverick, Lough Neagh or the Great Lake to mention most of them. There was also Saint Patrick's purgatory in present day County Donegal.

The headlands of the Antrim coast look rather similar to each other, and jutting out into the sea, look attractive at sunsets; these headlands are all volcanic in origin. Benbane Head, as seen from Dunseverick harbour, is a perfect example of this profile. Benbane means the "headlands of the goats". The water is calm in Dunseverick harbour proving safe moorings for two boats, whose registrations are CE58 and CE55, being the first and last letters of the port of registration at Coleraine.

The same families have always fished at Dunseverick harbour — the Gaults, the MacMullans, the MacClellands, the Wilkinsons, the McKays. The boats are Norwegian style clinker built dronheims which at one time were very popular with fishermen of the Antrim coast and were probably built in Kelly's boatyard in Portrush.

We have seen that Comgall reached Dunseverick Castle, an important foundation in the sixth century. Dunseverick is said to be the oldest castle in Ulster, deriving its name from the Gaelic "Dun Soihairce" meaning

"Severick's fort". Severick controlled that part of Ireland that lay north of a line drawn from Drogheda to Galway. At a later date Dunseverick was the terminus of the North-South Highway that ran from Tara, seat of the High-Kings, to Dunseverick; it was known as the "Sliabh Miaduachra". The O'Cahan occupied the castle from about 1237 until 1657.

A little up the coast lies the Causeway, which has numerous features that are difficult to photograph all at once. A typical photo of the basaltic columns shows these hexagonal pillars against a hill background. There are supposed to be 40,000 perpendicular columns of various sizes in the Causeway area. Today the National Trust controls the site. The basalt is said to have hit the sea very quickly, causing the lava to crystalize, thus forming the Causeway. It seems a likely explanation rather than Comgall's biblical account. The most famous of the Causeway formations is the honeycomb, featured in some magazines and tourist brochures and other publicity. Here the columns can be seen at their best — four, five, six, seven, eight and even nine sides can be seen.

The Giant's Organ is a formation reminiscent of the pipes of a grand organ. According to legend Finn Mac Coul is supposed to have built the organ for his son, who was a warrior poet. It is said that when the wind blew in the right direction, his music could be heard by the Grey Man, the legendary god of Fair Head, near Ballycastle. An exciting view is the Amphitheatre and Chimney Tops to the east of the Causeway. It is made up of several pillars towering above each other.

To the east also lies the Chimney Tops, the tallest of which is forty feet high. Oral tradition states that at the time of the Spanish Armada, the captain of the "Girona" mistook the Chimney Tops for Dunluce Castle and ordered his men to fire upon them and that the rebound drove the "Girona" onto a rock. It seems to have been an erroneous idea that the captain of the galleon "Girona" tried to fire at the Chimney Tops, mistaking it for Dunluce Castle.

The 28th October 1588 was a very stormy night, and the "Girona", with a damaged rudder and with over a thousand men aboard, was being driven along by a north west wind. It is possible that the captain was keeping as close to the coast as possible to avoid disaster. But the ship ran on to Lacada Point, a partially submerged rock stretching out into the sea. There were only eleven survivors. The place where the bodies were washed ashore is known as Port via Spaniah (the port of the Spaniards).

By the end of the seventeenth century the Royal Society in London began to take a scientific interest in the Causeway. Amongst the papers of the Society was one on the Giant's Causeway presented by Sir Richard Bulkley. Dr Lyster was also interested in 1693 and Dr Thomas Mollineaux, who died in 1733. Today there is a society established at the Causeway by the Moyle District Council.

Since Comgall's time the Causeway has been the subject of many paintings. Also of interest is the Wishing Chair, and Dr Johnson said that the Causeway was "worth seeing but not worth going see". However the Causeway was declared a World Heritage site in 1987. Alike in the sixth century, and the twenty-first century, there is something artificial about the columns and headlands of the Causeway; one can sit in the Wishing Chair, made out of the basalt, and make a wish.

There is Lord Antrim's Parlour, a circular group of pillars, which is supposed to have received its name when Lord Antrim entertained a party of friends there. There is also the Lady's Fan, named because of its shape. The Giant's Eyeglass, the Hawk's Head, the Priest and his Flock, the King and his Nobles, the Lover's Leap, the Four Sisters (four pillars), the Giant's Peephole and the Giant's Granary (a single column). There is a harbour near the columns. In ancient days fishing boats were drawn up at the port, and it might have been that Comgall landed there on his journey up the Antrim coast.

Today many boats are drawn up on the rocks, the boats being about twelve to fourteen in length, in contrast to the currachs of Comgall's age. The Gaelic name for the Causeway is "Port Noffer", and the small bays along the coast all have Gaelic names, for example Portnaboe (the cow's port), Port Granny (Sandy port), Port Reestan (the port of the king's dining room), Portnacallon (the girl's port), Port na Tober (port of the spring well), Port na Truin (port of sorrow) and Pleaskinn (the dry headland) and lots more. At length we come to Port Coon (the port of the harbour), which is a cave surrounded with mystery. The cave is forty feet high and boats can penetrate it for 150 yards. The interior resembles a Gothic cathedral, and a pistol can be fired for tourists, so that they can listen to the echo.

Chapter 9

The Mystery of the Cross

Perhaps in our day we learn to look back to the age of Comgall to recapture the atmosphere of ancient Christianity as opposed to the sophisticated beliefs of today. Ours is an age that rejects any sort of mystery; modern science seems to have "overcome" the fundamentalist beliefs that Comgall may have had. Modern science has put forward the idea that Christ was not crucified on a cross but upon a stake. Modern science has tried to explain away the mysteries of the ancient Celtic Churches and we are left with an unexciting form of the faith.

Some Protestants reject the fundamentalist character of the Eucharist. Christ realized that he was going to his death at Calvary, this was his mission, to teach the nations that he was the Messiah, but he did not regard Rome as the Antichrist for he had said that it was important to "render unto Caesar the things which are Caesar's and unto God the things that were God's".

Islam does not put forward a Messiah that had to die for the sake of the Earthly kingdom and the kingdom of Heaven. Comgall had a very special relationship with the Cross. He pictured his passion and the Lord's ability to overcome the fear of death. Crucifixion was the central act in Christ's story and in the life of the Church, both historically and in the present age. The cross was used to punish criminals at the time of the Roman Empire, and Christ had been declared a criminal by the Jews. Thus Comgall realized that Christ was right and the Jews were wrong. With the crucifixion of Christ, the modern Church was created and Christian history had begun. Christ was crucified next to two criminals, one of whom believed in him so that the wicked would be with him in paradise. Christ had come to proclaim spiritual Rome as the head of the earthly Church. Christ was following a way of life that Christ believed in; "A man can have no greater love / than to lay down his life / for his friends" *(John 15:13)*. Comgall's entire being was devoted to trying to understand Christ's passion, and he died trying to understand it, but for Comgall Christ literally had rose from the dead, to be the ultimate judge of those who had crucified him.

All around him in ancient Ulster Comgall witnessed suffering. The suffering of the wars between the petty kingdoms and the suffering of the first generations of Christians who struggled to keep Ireland attached to the faith.

Comgall was united with Christ as a result of his master's crucifixion. It was this central event that united the Church, an act acknowledged by the Pope as he claimed to speak infallibly about Christian doctrines and dogmas. Christ was cared for by his mother Mary, and the Church was to assign to her a very special role, for Jesus had been born of Mary as the result of the virgin birth. Comgall looked around him and everywhere he saw violence in Ulster — cattle raids, petty quarrels and the persecution of the Church. He looked to the Cross, to Christ's agony, as an example for all. The infant Jesus was aware that he would have to die in order to save mankind from the Antichrist. For Comgall the Antichrist of the sixth century were the barbarian invaders of Europe and Britain, with a possibility that Ulster might fall under their hammer. The Antichrist is talked about in the Book of Revelation, and the Messiah will come again to punish and judge those who followed him. From a very early age Jesus was gifted with the power of evangelization. He argued with the Scribes and Pharisees. It was this Jesus that Comgall took to his heart. Joseph and Mary marvelled at the intelligence of their son, and encouraged his career. Mary had given birth to Jesus; she also must have known that her son would die upon the Cross.

Comgall must have known that he too might have to die for his faith in the violent society of sixth century Ulster. The birth of Jesus is a great event. He was born in a manger, and Wise Men came from the East to pay him homage. He was recognized by those Wise Men as they talked about the Messiah in the Old Testament. Comgall also paid homage to Christ every Christmas and Easter, for the Church was a developing body, with Christ at its centre along with Christ's mother, the Virgin Mary. Comgall recognized the fact that God had unlimited love of his Creation; Christ had died that man should recognize the truth. As a man Christ had experienced also the emotions of an ordinary person. He had to face death, he had to overcome his fears. He had to undergo interrogation and punishment at the hands of the Roman authorities. Upon the Cross his side was pierced, upon the Cross his hands and feet were nailed into the Cross. Comgall took strength in God in his darkest moments when even a saint's faith might be shaken. Jesus was "King of the Jews"; in derision his life ended upon the Cross — "Father, father, forgive them, they know not what they do". Mary, his mother looked on, as Christ underwent his agony, and she might have been convinced that he would rise from the dead, to sit in judgement.

His career had started in Egypt at the height of the power of the Roman Empire. God had directed Mary and Joseph to leave Pharaoh's land and to travel to Jerusalem, so that the young Christ could start his mission. The first century world of Rome was a society based upon material values, rather like our own, a society in which faith was placed in the statues of the pagan gods. It was a society of low morals, tyrannous kings and Roman emperors. The Jews hated Jesus, even though he was the Messiah. A handful of disciples believed in him — Matthew, Mark, Luke, John and Paul to mention only a few, and some like Judas were to deny Christ. His favourite seems to have been Saint Peter, who as we have seen, may have been the first Pope. The Church teaches that we become closest to God when we experience pain, the pain of Jesus on the Cross. Suffering, of course, in the life of man is unavoidable. Comgall took up a life of meditation as a result of his ideas about his Maker. Comgall lived in a society where there was little treatment for ills. Now we live in a world that has been changed by modern medicine. Comgall could expect to die of a variety of diseases, and of course suffering brought him closer to God. The list of suffering is familiar — illness, mental anguish, old age, loneliness, heartbreak, unkindness, or the loss of a loved one.

Comgall realized the value of prayer; this Jesus taught was the true start of faith. Christ was there as a mediator between God and man and the Virgin Mary was also to be used in a similar capacity. Jesus prayed often, and those who followed him also placed their hope in prayer. It was said in Luke 9:22 that "The son of man is destined to suffer grievously and to be rejected / by the elders and chief priests and scribes / and to be put to death". The disciples taught that the death of Jesus had to be understood. Death was often mentioned by Christ in his travels in the Roman world. Peter had questioned Christ about death on the Cross. However pagans as well as Christians were just as convinced that there might be life after death, but in sixth century Ulster the powers of the pagans were in decline, and the visions of Christians more tangible. In a violent world Comgall realized that sometimes it was difficult to believe in God, for there was so much suffering. The Cross adorned the altars of the little churches, and this bears witness to suffering and to provide a spiritual cure. In the gospels Jesus had said that "If anyone wants to be a follower of mine let him renounce himself and take up his cross everyday and follow me". Christ's death, Comgall realized, was proof of God's love for us. The Church by the sixth century was still performing miracles; visions of Christ and Mary were claimed, just like in another age there would be pilgrimages to Lourdes and Fátima in Europe.

. The Virgin is sometimes pictured as weeping for the death of her son, and statues have exuded tears. Comgall should have been at the foot of the Cross during Christ's passion. Christ's death for sin meant that ordinary souls like Comgall could be saved, whereas the Jews had treated death upon the Cross as humiliating and the fate of the Antichrist. The disciples too must have realized that they would also face death upon the Cross for belief in Jesus, and this is what happened to Peter and Paul when they reached Rome. God had spoken to Comgall as he carried out his everyday tasks. He was with him in contemplation and prayer, he was with him in his journeys around Ulster and he would be with him at the time of his death.

Television for the modern Christian has revolutionized their lives. There was no fun in Comgall's Bangor, but today many Christians enjoy services on TV; for example Songs of Praise, performed for all denominations. Video has brought Christ into the hearts of many, where Bible reading alone is sufficient. The nearest thing Comgall had to a television were the illuminated manuscripts. The Church services at the monastery were basically the same as in a modern Catholic Church, Anglican or Roman Catholic. Television and radio bring to the modern Christian news of terrible events around the world. One can get into the minds of the Chinese and the Russians as Western Christians try to survive in a violent world. Comgall's age was also an age of great violence, and this is the theme that runs through the history of Christianity, Protestant or Catholic, in Ireland/ Ulster.

Television can teach the average Ulsterman the tenets of all the faith. Local history is popular on radio and television, and sometimes records the history of all the Churches. In the modern age Christians find it difficult to live with great disasters like that of the terrible events of September 11th in New York. This would have been a position that Comgall's simple faith struggled with. To a great extent the Church of Comgall has lived on in a violent world, a world in which faith is tested, but Christianity teaches that God will not try us with anything that we cannot live with or overcome. Comgall had to live with paganism and heresies that crept into the Church from the very start of Peter's mission. Since the end of the Second World War we have never lived in a more prosperous society in which the rule of law is obeyed. This is also true of the Catholic Church. Comgall lived in a very simple society in which there was no modern medicine and when life expectancy was short of three score years and ten. Today the Church looks back at man's inhumanity to man, and the career of Adolf Hitler, who was condemned by Pope Pius XII.

In ancient Ulster, although there was violence there is no word of the Antichrist at work. For Comgall the Antichrist reigned in the person of Attila the Hun, who sacked Rome in AD 410. Since the Second World War the Church and society are still recovering from the policies of the Third Reich. As in Comgall's day there was the position of the Jews in society and their right to live in a sovereign state, but say the Arabs, they are occupying Arab soil.

. For Comgall the Jews were the murderers of Christ, but Comgall's thoughts and attitudes were entirely evangelical, and he hated Judaism but loved Jews. Comgall is one of the great doctors of the Catholic Church, for it was an uplifting experience to become a priest. He was amazed at the healing powers of the very early Catholic Church. Comgall saw illness all around him, and he must have prayed frequently to God. Perhaps to a great extent modern man, like ancient man, is in search of God. Christianity is all about combating evil, and what is evil. Contraception was unknown in Comgall's age but it was essential to obey the Ten Commandments. As society has become more complex, so this is reflected in the faith, for example the involved faith of the Roman Catholic Church today. The creation of the mountains and oceans were great events to Comgall. In the words of the psalmist "They that go down to the sea in ships and occupy their business in great waters, these men see the works of the Lord, and his wonders in the deep" *(Psalm 107:23:4)*.

The Sea of Moyle or North Channel was a phenomenon of great power for both the Christian and the pagan. The gods had moulded the earth and were still performing miracles. Again the psalmist writes "If I take the wings of the morning / and dwell in the uttermost part of the sea, / even there they shall lead me / and the right hand shall hold me" *(Psalm 139:9:10)*. Darkness came to the North Channel and Belfast Lough and Comgall prayed to God to preserve him from evil. But the sea had a great peace, and was entirely created by God, and his spirit continually passed over the face of the waters. Comgall must have imagined the Red Sea and the Israelite flight out of Egypt, and he cast his mind back to the age of Finn Mac Coul (who had built the Giant's Causeway) in order to reach Scotland. On the front page of his daily prayer book, used by Comgall's monks, there printed in large letters (in Latin) the word "Pax", which means "peace". "The wind lashes the surface of the sea / and makes it rough and turbulent / but in the deep there is calm". This might suggest that Comgall was withdrawn from the problems of his age and everyday living. Around the life of Jesus is drawn a crown of thorns. Comgall tells his monks that they must learn to wear the crown of thorns if they are to find peace within themselves. Comgall was on an unending pilgrimage, for he recognized the part that destiny played in converting the Highlands of Scotland, something we have seen that was partly undertaken by Saint Columba. Comgall was on a pilgrimage through life and his vocation could be likened to that of the Salvation Army today. Our saint read the gospel of Saint John 17:3, and saw that God had said "And eternal life is this: to know the only true God".

Comgall grew in holiness and prayer for his life centred around the rule of the Bangor monastery, and at a later date the mission with Saint Columba to the Picts of the Northern Highlands of Scotland. He prayed and suffered because Christ had suffered; but he could not have suffered more than Jesus. His journey through life was guided by the crucified

Messiah, his mission was to always acknowledge and declare the truth. The disciples and apostles had suffered, and Comgall too might have to suffer death if Ireland was ever invaded by the barbarians, working from a European base.

Comgall had to face the unknown for he could die as the result of his evangelical activities. As a young man he had left all his friends to become Abbot of Bangor, and he must have longed for his childhood experiences at Magheramourne. It is not known how often he returned to his place of birth, even though he was making a name for himself throughout Ulster and Ireland. It had been said that going away is a kind of dying. Certainly Comgall did not like leaving his beloved Bangor to evangelize in Ulster and at length in Scotland. He one day would have to face the ultimate unknown — death. He prayed frequently so that his soul could be saved. He performed great works so that he could be saved. There was life beyond death, but the nature of this, Comgall did not know. He read in the Bible that in the last days the just would be resurrected. From the Church fathers he learnt that the Church would become very small and would become like the primitive Christian Church.

Comgall asked the question, "Why must death happen? Why should the ageing process take place?" However Comgall was sure that with the act of death lay new life, a new life with Christ. The dying saint would cry out to his Lord, as Christ cried out on the Cross on the first Easter. The human mind could not understand death. Like Christ Comgall would also be tempted — be tempted to leave the monastery and take up a place in the material world. Christ had fasted for forty days in the wilderness, so Comgall wanted to follow the example of his maker. Christ came face to face with the Devil, but he did not falter. The Devil might tempt Comgall, seeking out weaknesses in the saint's armour, but he had put on the full armour of God. His mother knew that Christ had fasted and that he had said "who is my mother and sisters and brothers". Many knew that Christ would have to face death for condemning the Jewish way of life. He had declared that he was the Messiah and that the Romans had to worship him. He was greater than the emperors, who also declared that they were divine. It was a far cry to the sixteen-year-old Christ, when he had started on his mission. Now at thirty-two, he was ready to carry his Cross to Calvary, where his mother witnessed a passion that she alone could understand.

Christ understood why he was suffering, for he claimed to be "King of the Jews". Comgall however at times of suffering was puzzled why God had brought anguish into the world, but Comgall was sure that his faith was like that of Saint Peter, who at length overcame his doubts of Christ to become, it is said, the first Pope. Comgall realized that the fulfilment of the law rested in Jesus's resurrection on that first Easter. Jesus had cried out from the Cross, "Into your hands, Lord, I commend my spirit".

Chapter 10

Slaves and Workers

As we have seen in a previous chapter, the royal and aristocratic kindreds multiplied rapidly because of polygamous marriages. This meant that a number of the aristocracy fell to the level of the peasant Irish. Sometimes they may have been capable of carving out new lordships. In the little townland of Magheramourne, where Comgall was born, slavery was a way of life. Slaves are known in the Bible, for example in ancient Egypt and the Roman Empire. The number of slaves a man had was an indication of his wealth. Saint Patrick had served his time as a slave at Slemish, but it is not known how tyrannous the institution of slavery was. It has been said that in the case of great princes, when their children and family multiplied, that their clients and followers were squeezed out, withered away and are wasted. It is not known what the percentage of slaves existed in relation to per head of population. Suffice to say that slavery was not only an important institution but an important way of life rather like full time employment means today.

In ancient Egypt slavery prevailed for many thousands of years, in comparison to the relatively recent institution of slavery in Ulster. Joseph and Mary had to flee from Egypt in fear of being reduced to slavery. Comgall expressed no desire to abolish slavery, for in Gaelic society in Ulster slaves may have been treated well. By the time of the Roman Empire, slaves were working in the mines and performing household tasks. They also rowed the large Roman galleys or warships. From earliest times slaves were an essential part of the workings of the family and Saint Patrick's mother and father may have had slaves.

If one wanted to make a name for oneself it was essential to study for the Church. The druids had been defunct and their power was limited by the efforts of the Catholic Church. The poets and bards had at last, in the sixth century, become largely extinct. A "mug" was a man slave and "cumal" a female slave. Looking back at history kings have had their

E

slaves and Ulster was no exception. Saint Patrick was perhaps a favourite slave of Lord Miliuc in the Slemish region and Dalriadian kingdom. By the Middle Ages the position of slaves in society was recognized by the law; they were an important part of society and they praised the rís and High-Kings. At Magheramourne if Comgall's family was wealthy there may have been slaves working in the fields, and catching fish in Belfast Lough as well as serving chiefs in the Laharna kingdom.

Slavery was common in Ulster until the age of Charlemagne in the ninth century. Slaves came from a variety of backgrounds and many of them were prisoners of war, as in the case concerning Saint Patrick. It seems incredible that the Church at one time or the other condemned the use of slavery. Nor is it known to what extent evangelists like Peter and Paul spoke out against the institution, or if they were concerned about it at all. However slaves were also part of the ancient kindred or chosen people. The word "Celtic" was primarily a linguistic term which is applied to closely related groups of Irish and Indo-European dialects. The slave was a lower order in sixth century Ireland. The Gaels of Magheramourne and Bangor Abbey considered themselves the cream of society; however there was no inclination towards regarding themselves as a master race. The Gaels of North Down were pleased with their society, and could boast now that it was Christian. Most of the slaves used in Ireland came from Britain, mainly the west coast. Comgall may have ventured out into the Irish Sea to land in Britain, where he observed the remnants of the once mighty Roman Empire. The journey would have taken him a couple of days and perhaps on the way he called in at Mona or the Isle of Man where the Manx race lived. Comgall would have run into slaves, still important after the fall of Rome. In Britain by the sixth century the Church had taken a firm root and Saint Augustine had set up a base for the Church at Canterbury in south east Britain. To some extent the Gaelic and British Churches competed with one another and there were many Irishmen that tried to set up a base in Britain, either for religious or political reasons. The British and Irish Churches have seemed to fundamentally believe the same sort of Christianity that prevailed at Rome.

Another source of slavery were peasants that sold their children at time of war. In a violent world it was difficult to approve of slavery. Presumably it was important for the master to treat his slaves well, for the abused slaves might run away and upset the economy of the tuatha or tribal kingdom. Like Patrick the slaves of Comgall's day toiled in the fields but the whip may not have been used. At times of famine mothers sold their children and the actual amount of these children may have been great. A female slave could be sold for three cows, but a male slave was perhaps of greater value than a female one. The men also toiled in the mines whilst the females tended to be employed in the master's or king's household. Slaves were baptized but did they believe in a Christ that had condemned them to drudgery? Certainly the Bible preaches the merits in belief in God, no matter what one's material or spiritual state might be.

If the Vikings reached Ulster before the sixth century, slavery would have been a very important institution, but we do not learn of any slaves that were taken to Norway to serve in the Viking cabins or to perform manual work. Rather the Vikings humbled the Christian by the use of violence, and a large part of Irish society was condemned to slavery. At a later date the Vikings themselves, as their power declined, were sent into slavery. Many Viking longships had rowed into the North Channel and Irish Sea, bringing into captivity many Christians. The Vikings of the sixth century, if we are to speculate that they had arrived in Ireland in the fourth century, were highly involved in the slave trade. However the humble Gaelic farmer in the Bangor and Magheramourne region did not make use of slaves. A rich man had many slaves, but it is not known if Comgall hired slaves to toil in the fields around his monastery. He himself thought that work was essential for the devout life, and so the monks toiled in the fields, perhaps disapproving of slavery. Certainly Irish slaves were not as well treated as slaves in Roman Britain, and this was an institution that did not die out with the sixth century. There might come a time when slaves would be unknown in the Gaelic world, but this was not to obtain for many centuries.

Today slavery is unknown to the civilized world, a monument perhaps to the influence of the Churches worldwide. Having been enslaved to Miliuc at Slemish, the young Patrick, as Comgall understood it, resigned himself to slavery as a Christian. Comgall realized the great saving virtue of Saint Patrick's career, and no doubt he moulded himself after the patron saint of Ireland. As far as slavery was concerned, there was little difference between the fifth and sixth centuries in Ulster. Comgall may have regarded slavery as one of the sins that the Catholic Church had to compromise with.

Hired labour was also used for menial work. By the eighth century the Cáin Domnarg (law of Sunday) lays down provisions for working men, so that if they work on the Sabbath they would forfeit a man's wages for a year. There was much menial work employed in the great monasteries. In lay society the menial workers might have been treated badly, but this seems incredible if a master wanted to keep his slaves from revolting against the powers that be. Payment for wages was made yearly and involved the handing over of livestock. Irish literature held itself aloof from pagan and Christian society and workers were held in contempt. It states that it was a waste of time hiring a slave, but I refer the reader back to another part, in which I claimed just treatment for Ireland's slaves.

A sage commented upon the state of slavery in Ulster; "It irks me that a serf's son should have converse with me". In Ulster there were workers, middle classes, its aristocrats and kings. It was a disgrace that a commoner's son should slay a king's son. The Gaels considered liberty as one of the prime attributes, even though they believed in slavery. To avoid slavery a Gael had to believe the tenets of the Catholic faith of Saint Comgall. They despised agricultural and mechanical pursuits, and these authorities claim that the Gaelic nobility looked down upon the peasantry and upon their servants with the greatest disdain.

Again it seems incredible that the menials and slaves were not treated relatively well, for we learn of no great slave or worker revolt in Comgall's Ulster and the Ireland of Saint Patrick. It is possible that between the first century AD and the sixth century the population of Ulster fluctuated considerably perhaps because of plagues and famine that tore apart the land particularly in the post Comgall age. The monks in the mid sixth century saw growth in agricultural and horticultural techniques. There was also the introduction of more sophisticated techniques. There was desert or wasteland in monastic place names, and the almost equally common "cluain" which may have meant pastureland won from the forest. This points to extensive colonization and the occupation of wasteland.

The woodlands were cleared, a process that may not have been completed by AD 800. The cultivation of land in Ireland lagged behind that of Britain, despite the overthrow of imperial Rome in the mid fifth century. There is a steady rise in population from the first century to the sixth century, mainly caused by the introduction of Christianity with its "make peace not war" manifesto. A great deal has to be learned about the organization of the farm in Ulster society in the sixth century. It is probable that the extent of a farm owned by a family was equal to the area of many present day townlands. It was centred around a ring fort, an area surrounded by a ráith or rampart of earth or stone, containing the dwelling house and the farm buildings, which were known as the byre, pigsty, sheep fold and calf fold. The enclosed area was the farmyard, and it was no bigger than an average Ulster farm today. Close by was the winter "macha" or milking yards. Some of these farmyards have been excavated, chiefly in the south of Ireland, for example the one at Cahiraveen, County Kerry which dates from the ninth or tenth centuries. These farmlands, including Ulster, were circular in plan, between eighty and ninety feet in diameter surrounded by high and massive dry built stone walls, broken by a single gateway. The dry-built house in the north was rectangular (20' x 25') built onto a circular beehive hut some fifteen feet in diameter. Around the walls of the farmland were two almost rectangular lean-to huts. Finds here include sirbles and ploughshares as well as evidence of milking and stock raising.

The size of the rath and the buildings doubtless fluctuated with the prosperity or poverty of the owners. It is also possible that there were poor inhabited smaller farms of their own. The houses did not need defending, making warfare the prerogative of the upper classes and aristocracy. In modern Ulster the farm still plays a leading role, for Ireland generally is an agricultural economy. Around about the raith or rath lay the arable ground, where the crops were carefully attended to. These fields contained an acre or two, and beyond lay the forest, moorland, rough land and rough mountain pasture, which were either owned privately or owned in common with a number of farms. Agriculture and farming in Ulster remained in a static condition on up to the Norman and Tudor conquerors.

The economy of Bangor Abbey was also geared to agriculture, and warfare was looked down upon even though there were inter monastic wars. The monks either fought in the wars themselves or hired mercenaries, perhaps the Vikings if the Norse had reached Ulster by the fourth century AD. Corn and milk formed the staple diet of the monastery. The monks grew cereals in the fields and Comgall oversaw the activities with prayers and exhortations to work and righteousness. Sometimes the corn crop was lost as the result of unfavourable weather. There were also smaller famines, smaller that the great famine of 1845-7 in the entire island. The monks were afire with warlike aspirations, for they often burnt or uprooted the enemy's corn, a practice that existed on up to the eleventh and twelfth centuries. Bangor Abbey is almost certain to have had a horizontal water mill, for monastic literature abounds with references to mills and milling. By the sixth century a complex body of customary law concerning the rights of the mills had been developed. The aíth or corn-drying is frequently referred to in literature, and points to the great importance of cereal growing. The monks ploughed the fields belonging to the abbey, and flax and vegetables were also cultivated.

The Irish word for a plough was cétch. Two types of plough seem to have been in use; a light two-ox plough without a coulter and a low, wheelless but heavy plough with a coulter. Evidence from the Lugore crannog or lake dwelling shows that a heavy plough capable of ploughing heavy soil was not in use throughout Ireland. The possession of a plough was venerated and even quite large farms had to pool their resources. The peasantry used a spade, a wooden instrument and shod with iron. Harrowing is mentioned in some of the law tracts. Harrows were drawn by horses. Ploughing was done in March and only one crop of corn was sown each year.

The scythe was unknown in Ireland, but was well known in Roman Britain, but the Irish showed no attempt to adopt this useful tool. Corn was harvested with the sickle. It was probably cut high up on the stalk near the ear, a practice well known in Europe. The remaining corn was either fed to the cattle or ploughed back into the soil. Corn was threshed with flails and beating sticks in a special barn, on a threshing floor or on any clean and dry part of the farmyard. Threshing and winnowing were considered to be the useful occupation of slaves. The grain, winnowed or unwinnowed, was stored in the barns in boxes and chests. There was also the fóir or straw rope granary.

All ancient civilizations have had their agricultural systems, the Roman example being the supreme example. Wherever Rome went her farmers and politicians followed. The agricultural economy of Ulster was basically little different from that of Rome. The early Christian communities of the first to sixth centuries, in Ulster and in Europe, saw the growth of monasticism and the agricultural system that was established wherever the monks went. There was much trade between Roman Britain and Ireland and this intercourse did not come to an end with the fall of Rome in the mid fifth century. The only difference was that the world of Rome was greater than that of the island of Ireland, but the Romans, as we have seen, may have had their eyes upon a conquest of the Irish tribes, especially those of the north east who were adjacent to Galloway in Scotland. The Romans had reached northern Britain at the time of the emperors Hadrian and Antoninus, both emperors having built walls named after them. The Romans did not reach the far regions of the Pretannic or British Isles. It was left to Comgall to reach the Picts of northern Scotland, the mission led by Columba of Derry and Iona, to the High-King of the Picts and his shamanists (a lower form of druidism). Everywhere in Britain, following the legions, came the Roman villa or farm, again on a bigger scale than the farms of Ulster but serving the same purpose. Both were basically forts. The walls of Bangor Abbey were meant to keep out what remained of paganism and the later Norse attacks. Comgall had to pray many times in order that his warlike instincts were forgiven.

Some eight types of cereals were known amongst the Gaels, and oats was the most common one, followed by barley, wheat and rye. At various places of excavation in Ulster traces of cereal have been found. Wheaten bread was considered a delicacy and was eaten by the upper classes on special occasions. Much of the grain grown was eaten as porridge and a great deal of it was used in the manufacture of ale. There were inbgort or vegetable gardens. A vegetable called caineun was eaten, along with imus or celery, which was grown on ridges or drills. Foltchep, a variety of onion, was also cultivated. There were also some top roots grown but whether they were parsnips or carrots it is not known. Peas and some vegetables of the cabbage family were also cultivated. There was crem (wild garlic) and other wild plants that were also eaten. Vegetables and corn were grown on ridges, the length and breadth of which was governed by the laws. It appears that the Gaels were familiar with the technique of manuring. Apple trees were also cultivated, and Saint Patrick and Comgall may have planted some of these trees. According to the laws, a tenant who is attacked in war is entitled to compensation for the apple trees which he had planted. Bangor Abbey is almost certain to have had an orchard, and the monks would have lived off the fruit. In the diet apples were supplemented with nuts, wild fruit and berries.

The fields of North Down and the rest of Ulster were emerald with the frequent rainfall. On the land cattle, sheep and pigs were reared. Land was measured in the number of corn it could support, and legal compensations were reckoned in terms of cattle. A man's standing was reckoned with the number of cattle he possessed. The cow was the most immediate form of mobile wealth for raiding, for granting fiefs to clients and for paying one's debts. Cattle were pastured on the rougher land and herded by youths. The swineherd has been regarded as a sacred person. Transhumance — the herding of cattle into the mountains — was practised. In the mountains the women attended to making buttermilk. There were also summer milking places in the hills. Only a limited amount of winter fodder was available. If the winter was long and cold there would be great losses of stock. There were also great frosts and falls of snow which the people and the monks had to cope with. Cattle were kept mainly for milk and not for beef. Milk and its products, curds, cheeses, milk drinks and preparations supplied a great deal of the Irish diet. Milk was drunk fresh (lemlacht), thickened (bainne clabair), soured and skimmed (dranmce), and whey of various kinds was considered a delicacy. Milk was also widely consumed in the form of curds (gruth). Gruth may also have been an impressed cheese like modern cottage cheese. Curds are mentioned in the law tracts as eaten with bread, as food rent, and also compensation for minor trespasses. The generic name for cheese is cáis, a borrowing from the Latin word casens, and has led to the belief that cheese was unknown in Ireland until the introduction of Christianity (before the fifth century?). Fáiscre grotha was a cheese made out of curd, pressed in a mould and probably eaten fresh. Tanay was a round hardy dry cheese made of skimmed milk and pressed in a mould. Táth was a cooked cheese made of sour milk curds. Máethal was a smooth textured, soft-bodied cheese, round in shape, and mulchán appears to be a cheese made from buttermilk curds.

Churns were manufactured from oak or other hard wood and were often large stave-built vessels, wide at the bases and narrow at the top. Churning was done with a dash-churn. Butter was buried in the bogs in order to keep it sweet over long periods.

Pigs were raised in small quantities and were fed on fodder and grass in the woods. Sheep were raised for their wool, but a boiled sheep was considered no mean food. A ninth century work stated "do not dress elegantly unless you possess sheep....for elegant dress without sheep is a crime in the gathering of the world". Sheep were mainly the responsibility of the women and were frequently left out of doors regardless of the weather. Losses of sheep because of the winter snows and frost are also mentioned in the annals. Sheep were also housed in folds during the winter and there are occasional references to stall feeding. Irish sheep were generally black, but white sheep were considered superior. Sheep were also used as milk-producers, as they were in various other European countries.

Horses were kept, but not for very heavy work. Oxen were used for ploughing, for drawing heavy carts and for other heavy work. Oxen were also used to draw hearses. The horses seem to have been raised on the mountain pastures and were broken in when they were fully grown. British horses were highly prized, and they were imported for breeding purposes. Horse meat was sometimes served at Comgall's Bangor, and also in lay society, but it was not generally eaten. The Church endorsed many of the aspects of the Gaelic or Brehon laws.

Chapter 11

The Mother of God

The Virgin Mary is a very important figure in Catholic Christianity, and the basis for belief in her can be traced back to the gospels and other works in the Bible. All generations have praised and prayed to her. Comgall had a very special kind of relationship with Mary, for using her as a mediator between himself and Christ. However the Bible does not mention Mary as the mother of God, but as the mother of Jesus. Mary was born of Elizabeth, and the conception was immaculate, i.e., Mary was conceived without original sin. As a result of the Virgin birth, and after the death of Christ, the Virgin Mary was assumed into Heaven, and has taken her place alongside the saints, Christ and his Father.

We know very little about the historical Mary. Mary is a reflection of Jesus's mission. She gave birth to Jesus in a manger for there was no room for her and Joseph in the inn. Mary is the new Eve. The Bible says very little about Mary's nature; all we know is that she was the mother of Jesus, and by reckoning the mother of God.

In Comgall's Bangor Abbey there would have been statues raised to the Blessed Virgin. Their colour lit up the interior of the Abbey. Mary is pictured as a young woman and tears exude from her eyes on statues, for she perpetually cares for her crucified son. She is intrinsically involved in the life and work of Jesus. An angel bore the message that she was the chosen one, the one to have given birth to the Christ. Mary must have known that God had a very special role for her. Both she and Joseph had read the Old Testament and in it it was proclaimed that a Messiah would come. The couple kept all this in their hearts, and they left Jesus as a young man, to preach in the synagogues, claiming that he was the Christ and that she the Virgin Mary was his mother by an act of God. The angel must have told Mary of the divinity of Jesus for in the coming ages the Messiah would be venerated. But the Jews were to reject Jesus, who claimed that he was "King of the Jews". They demanded the death penalty,

73

but the Roman authorities could find no fault in him, so Pontius Pilate sentenced him to death against his better judgement. The divinity of Jesus must have become evident when he was in his early years, but he was to say that all were his sisters and brothers, and he called Mary "woman". Jesus did not state that Mary was his mother, and it appears that she was relegated to the role of an earthly mother. Today the Protestant Churches consign Mary a symbolic role in the birth of Jesus. It is not necessary to uphold the Virgin birth for Jesus was a man like anyone else. Mary and Joseph however are not above the law even though they presented Jesus in the temple, offering two little doves. Mary is the bearer of Christ's message for the world, and she lives according to the law. Mary and Joseph must have wondered what would eventually come of their son. The ancient Jewish laws governed the relationship between man and woman in society. The essence of the law can be traced back to Moses's experience on Mount Sinai, where he was given the Ten Commandments from God.

Comgall must have treasured the career of Moses, for must not Bangor Abbey have lived in accordance with the Torah. In reading the whole Bible, Comgall was not only acquainted with the history of Israel, but also with the history of the World. Civilization grew up in the Near East and God revealed himself to the prophets and was now revealing himself to the Virgin Mary. There were also the writings of the Latin and Greek Church fathers, who recorded the role played by the Virgin Mary. By the age of Comgall at Bangor, sixth century worship of the Virgin Mary had become a complicated business.

It is not known exactly at what date Mary worship became known in the Catholic Church. Certainly at the time of Peter and Paul, there is very little mention of her. In the Bible, as we have seen, she was called the "mother of Jesus", the Church making the assumption that she was the mother of God. Mary was not overprotective of Jesus; she let him go his own way, for she was aware that she had given rise to the Virgin birth. She expected no reward for this, and she did not expect that she would be assumed into Heaven. The maternal figure is well known amongst the many civilization that have worshipped her and believed in God. Christianity also grew up at a time when other great religions were taking shape, i.e., Islam. No doubt the Old Testament borrowed from these and other religious phenomenon, like the numbers ten, seven and three being common: the Ten Commandments, the seven days of Creation, and the three persons of the Trinity. God however had no plan to make Israel a world power. With the coming of Mary worship however God meant that Christianity should dominate the world and heading this crusade were the statues of Christ and his mother.

By the sixth century the Irish Church had become Marian, and Comgall grew up in a Church that was similar to the Roman Catholic Church today. Comgall saw no conflicts in worshipping Christ's mother, nor for having statues of Jesus and Mary within Bangor Abbey. Comgall said his prayers to Jesus, and Mary played an important role. Comgall must have searched the Old and the New Testament in order to justify his belief in Mary. Mary and Joseph gave Christ a conventional education. Being the Messiah did not mean that he should receive any special treatment. He had come to humble himself in front of his mother. He said to her that he was the Messiah and that she was his earthly and spiritual mother. From an early date Jesus was cut out to be a very special person. He was not arrogant and he took after his mother, for Mary was humble in the sight of God. She had no idea that he would rebel against the Jewish authorities or that he would face death on the Cross.

The Jews did not like Jesus and only some of them followed him, e.g., Saint Peter, Saint Paul and the other disciples. Christ preached to the multitudes and his mother looked on, gradually realizing that he would take on a Messianic role. It was the common person that admired and followed Jesus; it was the ordinary person that would venerate Mary, believing that she was the mother of God, and that God spoke to Jesus as he approached Calvary. Mary must have realized that she would play an important role at the crucifixion. The death of Jesus meant that Mary was further blessed for now came the all important fact of her assumption into Heaven. Mentally and symbolically Mary also died on the Cross with her son. She urges the people to accept him as the Messiah — she talks about her divine son and does not stand in the way of his progress towards Calvary. She must have known that Jesus would incur the wrath not only of the Jews but also the Roman imperial authorities. Comgall was aware that Christ had urged the Jews to render unto Caesar the things which are Caesar's and unto God the things that were God's. They however may not have considered him a threat to the state for it was the Jews that demanded his death. The Jews regarded Jesus as a deserter and a false prophet. He claimed to be the Son of God and the long awaited Messiah of the Old Testament. Mary realized that Jesus from the start of his mission, would proclaim that he was the Son of God. Her son demanded that as God he should be accepted by both the Jews and the Gentiles. Mary had no idea that within a hundred years of Jesus's birth that Christianity would have spread throughout the Roman Empire. Mary and Joseph regarded the Roman state as a tyrant, but Jesus had exhorted unto the people to "render unto Caesar". Little is known of the relationship between the Virgin Mary and Jesus. Jesus's divinity is doubted by modern scholarship which consigns to Jesus an earthly role and simply leader of the first Christians. The divinity of Christ is questioned and denied. Jesus was emphatic however, for he claimed to be God, King of the Jews. The early Church in Ulster undoubtedly made images in order to draw closer to God, but this was breaking God's law that had stated that it was a sin to make unto one's self any graven image. The Eastern Orthodox Church as well as the

Roman Church, in the past, has laid much emphasis upon statues of the Virgin Mary and icons. Catholics claim that images help them to understand their faith. In the twenty-first century the situation is little different, with the Evangelical Churches rejecting the use of images to understand God. Comgall had a very good understanding with Christ, along with the Virgin Mary, but most of all he held fast to his relationship with Christ, who was the Christian Messiah. Comgall had no conflict in making unto himself an image of Christ or of the Virgin Mary. He would site biblical references for his faith. There are references to images in the Bible where God punished those who worshipped the golden calf.

The worship of images goes back far into the history of mankind. The Jews however used no images of any kind, and they condemned their use in Christianity. For Comgall the making of images took second place in regard to prayers to God. An image was there to assist in prayer, and the image itself was not worshipped but what it represented. Some Protestant Churches today receive the idea of images, even though they claim a fundamentalist view of the Scriptures. On 1st November 1950, the feast of All Saints, in the presence of a crowd of about one million, and surrounded by 700 bishops, Pius XII defined the dogma of the assumption of the Virgin Mary into Heaven. We have seen in previous chapters that belief in the assumption was nothing new and that it has a first place in the early Church. For centuries the feast of the assumption had been celebrated on 15th August. It was a tradition that was common to both East and West. Pius XII had stated that Mary reigns in Heaven with her son, her body and soul shining with heavenly glory.

Mary became Queen of Heaven. The Virgin Mary was free from any original sin, either at birth or at the point of death. God then proclaimed that she was Queen of all Creation. Comgall understood, in his study of the first few centuries of Christianity, that Mary was received body and soul into Heaven. Perhaps before the sixth century the role of Mary was being defined by the Catholic Church. Mary was higher than a saint, although she was not part of the Trinity of the Father, Son and Holy Spirit. Pius XII bestowed upon the Virgin Mary a very special role not only in this life but in the one to come. The Assumption of the Virgin Mary has been well portrayed in art (images), and Comgall no doubt had a painting of this glorious event. Comgall prostrated himself in the presence of Mary, who always had faith in her divine son.

It was Mary's privilege to help to define the faith that she had experienced. This was her faith from the very beginning. She carried within her her secret calling. It was Mary's privilege to be assumed into Heaven, and Comgall had complete trust in her. Mary, like her divine son, were to live for ever more. It was important that Comgall believed in a life after death, a life lived in the company of the Virgin Mary and her son. The ordinary person was also privileged to know Mary, for all sins were forgiven by an act of faith in the doctrines and dogmas of the Catholic Church. Mary had no idea when she would die; perhaps this might happen shortly after the death of Jesus. The Bible gives no indication of when the death of the Virgin Mary would take place, and it only states that she was assumed into Heaven, according to the writers of the Latin and Greek Church fathers. Jesus had said to Mary that he had many brothers and that Mary's role in the crucifixion had been ordained from the beginning of time. Mary was aware that she was born to cut out an important role in the Christian life of the Roman Empire and ancient world in general.

By dying the Virgin Mary, like Christ, was entering a new life. What Heaven was like, no one in biblical times knew. Man had apparently been created in the image of God, and Mary's role was that of a woman being alongside that of her son. Comgall himself knew that some day he would also die, and in so doing he might be received into Heaven by Christ and the Virgin Mary. Belief in the role of Mary was essential for salvation, an attitude witnessed by the Church through the ages. However the Scriptures tell us very little about the assumption of Mary, for this we rely on the writings of the Church fathers and the teachings and guidance of the popes. Nor is it clear when Mary worship appeared in the Church. As stated this was a phenomenon of the early Church, an age in which the faith was preserved pure and simple. However Saint Comgall was living 500 years after the crucifixion of Christ, and there is no reason to suppose that he challenged the basic principles of the Church, the Church of Rome. The Catholic Church, Comgall's Church, lay great emphasis upon traditions, but Christ warned about this as being against the Bible. He said that many learned theologians perverted the word of God through their traditions.

The assumption of Mary is a major event within the Church whilst other views seem to have little biblical foundation. The assumption of Mary is mentioned in the non biblical books, some of which are accepted by the Roman Catholic Church as part of the liturgy of the Bible. Comgall realized that Mary was the mother of all human beings, by virtue of her place in Heaven alongside God and Jesus Christ. She is the mother of the converted and those ignorant of Christianity. She is also the mother of all heretics.

To understand the faith of the Catholic Church it is essential to understand the role of Mary — this Comgall did, for his career was indeed very Catholic. In the modern age there has been much Protestant reaction to the Papal position on the assumption of the Virgin Mary, but there have also been conversions to the Catholic faith and to the image and icon of Mary, for example Cardinal Henry Newman in the nineteenth century. Comgall believed that the Church had a mission of truth and this could only be achieved by reading the Scriptures and the writings of the Church fathers. Mary held an ecumenical faith for she recognized all Christian faiths as a manifestation of the divine. Mary is pictured as lamenting the death of her son, in statues and in icons or pictures. Mary glorified womanhood, and the faith throughout the ages has carried on this message.

Comgall's nuns were brides of Christ, their foundations growing up separately from the Bangor Abbey community of monks. From the very beginning the role of women in the Church is recognized, and this holds true today. For every nun, Mary acts as a universal mother. Therefore the cult of Mary has perpetrated itself through the ages. Mary has appeared in apparitions to many people since the first Easter. She has appeared at Knock in County Mayo and she no doubt appeared to the devout Comgall as he prayed within his monastic walls. He said that the cult of Mary was not idolatry, but an integral part of Christian worship. The "Hail Mary" is recognized in the Bible and as we have seen the Bible described Mary as the mother of Jesus, though not the mother of God. Modern criticism, as in the Protestant camp, argues that God could not possibly have had a mother, for God is a monotheistic being as taught by the Jews in the Old Testament. Prayers made on the rosary or holy heads can also be traced far back into antiquity, and the High Anglican Church meets here in common ground with that of the Roman Catholic Church. To the fundamentalist Presbyterian the Catholic Church of Comgall was and is full of errors. The first error being the assumption of the Virgin Mary into Heaven. Then follows other Catholic theories like that of transubstantiation and the infallibility of the Pope. The most famous appearance of Mary was that of Lourdes in France. In 1858 a revelation was given to Bernadette Soubirous. Another famous revelation occurred at Fátima in Portugal. The Catholic Church of Comgall had no hesitation in proclaiming Mary — hail holy queen, but in the twenty-first century there is perhaps as much emphasis given to belief in Mary as to the role of Christ. The Protestant Churches are emphatic. Mary was only the mother of Jesus, and there was no assumption into Heaven.

Chapter 12

Sex and Marriage in Ancient Ulster

The term "ancient Ulster" generally covers the period from the dawn of history to the Middle Ages. There were no written records — if there were records they have long since disappeared. Ulster was not a classless society; on the contrary it was divided into several distinct classes as any society must have been in order to survive.

The legal system of ancient Ulster is something totally different than it is today and it grew up from the system of the ancient Gaelic tribes. Generally speaking anyone that committed a crime against another had the penalty decided by rank and worth of the plaintiff. Here we come across the 'enechlan' or honour price. Any crime or misdemeanour could be termed as an offence against a man's or a woman's honour and the penalty was calculated by its seriousness. There was another penalty called 'dire' or 'corpdire', a form of atonement. The honour price of a rí was seven cumals or female slaves, while his wife was half this. Murder was considered a very serious offence and the penalty for this was known as "éraic". The penalty was several cumals for every freeman, irrespective of rank. For bodily injuries the "éraic" was obtainable by the injured man or woman. Éraic was often considered as "blood money".

The Brehon laws have given us some idea as to man/woman relationships. The Greek word "fer" (man) derives from the Latin virtus, which means strength. The Gaelic word for woman is benignites (kindred) in the Latin. Strength from the man and kindness from the woman were expected in accordance with the Brehon laws. The status of women in Comgall's Ulster was very high, higher than the role of women in the Roman Empire. It is thought that this was the case due to the social system that existed before the coming of the Gaels. During the many invasions of the tuatha or tribal regions, men and women held equal rank. Crimes and misdemeanours against a person's sexual wellbeing and rights are treated for in the Brehon laws. There is no mention anywhere of barbarian crimes,

79

for example the removal of the female breasts or for castration in men. If a man's penis was cut off he was entitled to two types of compensation for his loss. The full honour price had to be paid and in addition to this the atonement called corp-díre in full. The term used for penis in this tract is uidim, and this term could also mean "implement" or tool. If a man's scrotum was cut off full compensation was payable. If a man's left testicle only is removed against his will the full body price is payable. If a man in holy orders was castrated or his penis removed, there was a special price payable, but it was noted a priest, as a celibate had no need for his reproductive organ.

There was the crime of rape. In one case a woman could be violated sexually by violent possession, another way was to violate her while she was asleep and could not put up any resistance. Rape could occur as the result of the slaying of a king, leaving his daughter vulnerable, but the woman could react violently, often biting off the nails of her assailant. There was the honour price of a rapist, firstly there was a heavy fine affecting the rapist's relations, and they all participated to pay. The woman's relations also saw that justice was done. If the assailant did not pay the fine a debt collector might arrive at his doorstep. If he did not pay after a period a lot of his cattle could be confiscated. There was no question of imprisonment or corporal punishment of any kind.

Comgall, although a monk and abbot, was also a sexual being, embracing celibacy, said to be a higher condition in society. He may not have approved of society's attitude to rape, for he could quote Scripture. A rapist should not only be severely punished in society, but should also be consigned to the fires of Hell. Ancient society was very permissive, and we learn about worship of the golden calf in the Bible and how the god-fearing often turned away from God to worship idols, to fornicate and to practice homosexuality. Comgall's Ulster at the very grass roots must have been quite permissive, for it was difficult to convert the lower classes by virtue of numbers, but conversions often took place at open air meetings when Comgall would preach the gospel.

Comgall lived in an Ulster when the old pagan ways were finally passing and when a man should have only one wife. Celibacy was treasured by both the East and West in Europe, and only in Ireland by the sixth century was polygamy practised. Comgall was aware that he was growing up in a potentially violent society, in a society that was wreaked by internal wars between the tuatha, in a world in which he was obliged to bless the often violent kings, but who professed Christianity and perhaps other religions. In West Rome priests never expected to be celibate along with the bishops and archbishops. The Pope himself was also celibate, but eventually in the Greek Orthodox Church priests were allowed to marry, although the higher orders remained unmarried. Comgall grew up under the defunct West Rome system, and as such his beliefs and actions reflected the society of that period. However there is no biblical mandate for the celibacy of the clergy. It is not stated anywhere that a man should be celibate for the sake of the kingdom of God. However many of the great heroes of the church, for example Saint Paul, were celibate. Today celibacy is not practised by the Church of Ireland, and this communion has no monasteries, unlike the Church of England, which professes monasticism. Monasticism died out in Ireland with the coming of the Reformation, for numerous monasteries were sacked. Other sects like that of Presbyterianism are against the monastic system.

There were also other sexual misdemeanours which carried an honour price. It was stated that if a man shaved off the hair of a woman in order to seduce her, he incurred a full honour price. This was a very old custom and some think that it had its origins in Islam. The putting of one's hand under a woman's clothing in order to seduce her was known as "meblaigne," which also means "shaving". Incest was regarded with horror. In ancient times the King of Ulster, Conor Mac Nessa, had twenty-one sons in all. He was discontented with his many wives and it is said that he slept with his mother when he was drunk. The gods punished him and only three of his sons survived into manhood.

Homosexuality is not mentioned much. Masturbation was also condemned and it was regarded as self polluting, in Gaelic "truailliu". It was also known as Iám-chairdes, which literally meant "manual sex". Wooing has very little mention in the Irish law tracts and we must look to the storytellers of the sixth century to fill in the gaps in history. Comgall, like Columba, wanted to limit the power of the storytellers. Wooing was considered to be very important to the bards and poets. They formed a class of their own, "theaos dána", the "literary class". The Brehon laws had set out the grounds for legally held marriages and under what conditions.

It was men, so Comgall believed along with the pagans, who had to initiate the act of love. The lawyers distinguished seven different cases; firstly a barren man which indicated someone contracting marriage when it was already apparent that he could not procreate. On these grounds the act of marriage could be annulled by the authorities. The Christian position throughout the ages is clear from reading the Bible. Man should only have one wife and she was to be regarded with respect. The first Eve dwelled in the Garden of Eden which must have been very like the orchards of Bangor Abbey and North Down. Divorce, so the Church later taught, was only granted on grounds of adultery, a system cherished by the popes. Impotence on account of a party is not grounds for divorce like the pagan system. Then secondly there is the case of an unmarried man, if the man remained impotent. Thirdly there was a man in holy orders, as we have seen. Fourthly there is the case of a Church man, meaning a bishop, which has also been discussed. Fifthly there is the case of a rock man who had no land. The laws applied generally to what were called the Feni, all freemen, whether of noble or freemen status. Sixthly there is the case of a very fat man; the law explains that a fat man may not be able to perform the sexual act. Lastly there is the "claenán", meaning perverted little wretch. In ancient Ulster the woman was regarded as the weakest sex, but great things, like the bringing up of children, were expected of her.

With the establishment of the Christian Church in Ulster in the fifth century (or before) the Gaels were exposed to a totally different system that was based on the legal system, of the overthrown Roman Empire. It is not known how quickly the new legal system took root or how long it took for the Gaels to become converted. It is thought that the Church and the druids were at first sympathetic to each other's systems. To make conversations men like Comgall had to compromise with the pagans, for the simple Ulster man could neither read or write. It was useful to make images, statues and paintings to portray the faith. Comgall believed the Christian who committed adultery should do a year's penance for it. After a year he should come and be absolved by a priest, when he had brought witnesses to his penance. Any virgin, vowed to chastity, who took a lover, should be excommunicated until she is converted. After her conversion and the dismissal of the adulterer she should do penance and afterwards must not live in the same house or village as the man. The Brehon laws were liberal about divorce, but Comgall's view was stern. Any woman who has taken a man in a decent marriage and who leaves him to go with an adulterer is excommunicated. Also if any man gives his daughter in a decent marriage and if she then loves another man, and he accepts a dowry for her, both should be shut out of the Church. Any cleric who is seen without a tunic and who does not cover his body, and whose hair is not cut after the Roman manner, and whose wife walks about with her head uncovered, should be despised by the laity and separated from the Church. A monk and a virgin should not lodge in the same hostelry nor travel in the same chariot from village to village, nor carry out continual conversation with each other. The average Gael must have thought that the new system of Christianity was quite stern and not open to compromise, but Comgall had a definite and moral message. The figure of Christ and the Virgin was welcomed as a refuge from the bleaker aspects of Gaeldom and its druids. As before the fifth century the Gaels had heard of the Pope and his Christian Church — perhaps they may have wished to be influenced by the Roman pontiff, for Christianity preached goodwill towards all men and forgiveness of sins. The Church represented peace in Comgall's age, although it became intolerant with the coming of the Middle Ages. At length the Roman emperors demanded that their subjects should follow the Church and the popes started to adopt an attitude of infallibility as the centuries wore on. The attitude of the popes in regard to marriage was the same as the Church's position in the twenty-first century — strict belief about divorce and all other sexual relations between men and women. Christ was celibate, and he carried on no sexual relations with women, although his message was for both sexes.

Divorce was tolerated by the ancient Gaelic laws. These laws were extent in Christian times, and frequent reference to the Church confirms this. Two categories of people in regard to divorce were recognized by the Brehon laws. In the first category the departing did not incur any penalties or have to pay any special compensation to the woman he was leaving, except the usual division of property and wealth. The second category is that of women who have acquired a right to divorce their husbands and be fully compensated in all respects for their troubles. Divorce was a "bleaker" affair and these are some of the categories. If a man became ill, making the marriage impossible, divorce was granted, and also if separation was brought about by some disease. If pilgrimage was made by one of the partners, then divorce was an option. If there was some serious physical blemish or injury which was not cured or incurable, in the opinion of a Brehon, the divorce was granted. If a man left his homeland to seek a friend or avenge an agression or any such reason, divorce was granted.

Loss of sanity was grounds for divorce. If the parties are agreed, they could separate without penalty in order to form another union. Death was another reason and this was necessary to safeguard the position of the other partner. In the second category divorce is granted when a woman whose husband circulates a false story about her amongst the people. This was a serious vilification of his wife by a husband and automatically gave her the right of separation. If the husband circulates a satire among her neighbours and friends, she can leave him without blame to herself. Any woman that has been struck a blow which blemishes herself is also entitled to separation and to divorce. If a man becomes homosexual or is a homosexual, divorce was granted. If a woman is rejected because of another, she was also entitled to divorce. A woman who is denied sexual intercourse with her husband, was also a candidate for divorce. If a husband gives his wife a "philtre" — a drug of some kind — to induce her to sleep with him, this forms grounds for divorce on her side. If a woman is denied adequate food by her husband, then there was grounds for divorce. A woman who deserts her husband without good cause was treated as a fleeing thief. If a woman is blamed for the break up of a marriage she had to return all the "coibcle" presents she had received from him, and her kindred must also do the same. If the marriage had been for a considerable time the amount returned was very high. If it was the man who was responsible for the breaking up of a marriage, the whole "coibcle" was retained by her. Often a man or a woman would openly commit adultery, making the fines and honour-price high.

In discussing adultery it is important to consider the difference between a small and a serious offence. In modern society liberalism has triumphed in Ulster with divorce available through the courts, but with Southern Ireland adopting a conservative stance. Many women make their way north to Northern Ireland to obtain divorce through the courts. The position in the south is because of the conservative policies and attitudes of the Roman Catholic Church.

This was a situation that obtained in Comgall's Ulster, where the Catholic Church gradually spread its influence into secular matters. In ancient Ulster where there were serious penalties for some sex offences, the man would have to give the woman a "coibche". Wherever a woman received this sign of intent the man must give his "cémuinta" back to her a "coibche", as well as her honour price. Sometimes the woman would elect to stay in the house of the man she had been unfaithful to and in regard to this there was compensation.

Comgall's Ulster was very liberal in regard to sex in the pagan sector, but the Gaels may not have understood the Catholic Church's attitude, although this did not stand in the way to conversion to the faith. Comgall's sixth century Ulster saw the rise of religion and the end of paganism with the overthrow of liberal attitudes towards sex. All the great religions and pagan beliefs have had a definite role to play in regard to sexual matters. In the Bible we learnt that homosexuality was condemned; God would punish the wicked, perhaps by death; "Thou shalt not commit adultery". A man should only have one wife. Perhaps the laws concerning adultery and contraception may relax in the South of Ireland bringing the Catholic Church into conformity with British beliefs. The Church can site Scripture in regard to her conservative attitudes. Peter, said to have been the first Pope, believed that it was essential to have only one wife, an attitude reflected in the career of the apostles and disciples of the up and coming Church of Rome.

Both Judaism and Christianity share what might be termed as intolerant attitudes towards sex, especially in the sexual attitudes of young people. The Pope instructed Comgall's Gaelic Church that as an abbot and monk he should remain celibate, a tradition cherished by the Latin Church. The sixth century Church condemned all forms of permissiveness in Ulster and the other Irish kingdoms. Modern societies in the West seem to have forsaken their allegiance to Christianity, especially in the Catholic Church. In the Lutheran Church attendances are down by 50%, whilst the Protestant Churches have forsaken their fundamentalist beliefs and stern attitudes to sex, in their attitudes to divorce and contraception. It is said that in the last days the Church will again become a small and persecuted body, that the Antichrist will reign and that Jesus would return to judge the wicked and other sinners. "Many there are but few are chosen". The world would not be destroyed by water, but perhaps Comgall looked out across the waters of Belfast Lough, observing its peace. In this latter day world the Gaelic Church had started to build a firm foundation.

Chapter 13

Hunting, Fishing and Seafood

Life in Comgall's Bangor Abbey was rather like that of the life of an ordinary Gael. Reference in the annals are made to hunting, but these writings give us little indication of the day in the life of the tribesmen at North Down. Waking started early, perhaps at four o'clock in the early hours of the morning at which time the monks had said their prayers and perhaps celebrated mass or holy communion. Comgall realized the value of manual labour for the soul and he would toil in the fields and go hunting with his fellow brothers. Manual labour and walking brought Comgall closer to Jesus and to the Virgin Mary. Deer was hunted in the flatlands along the shores of Belfast Lough. Comgall would travel south to the kingdom of Mourne, which seemed to have remained Christian after the visitation of Saint Patrick. Comgall would have made this journey by currach or small skin covered craft, reaching the Mournes, in a day. Alternatively if he wished to travel inland, his journey would have taken him a little longer.

The monks used their bows and arrows in order to kill deer, which they ate with great respect. Bangor Abbey was surrounded with water in the north by Belfast Lough, to the east by the Irish Sea and to the south by Strangford Lough. To the west lay Belfast and the Lagan valley. Deer traps have been found and representations of these are not uncommon. Deer bones in small quantities have been found in Ulster and at dwelling sites, which can be dated back between 700 and 1000 BC. Other authorities had pointed out that the stags of Ulster were so fat that they were unable to elude their hunters. The wild boar was also hunted. The monks praised God that they had a plentiful supply of meat and cereal in the lands surrounding the abbey. As the monks and Gaels cleared the forests, the boars became extinct by the twelfth century, the age of the Norman invasion of Ireland, and the setting up of the kingdom of Ulidia, covering most of present day Antrim and Down. The flesh of both the boar and the deer, according to a ninth century monastic text, was held to be much inferior to the flesh of domestic animals. The lands of North Down were fertile in comparison to the rock lands in south east of Down, and the Mourne Mountains looked out across the Irish Sea to the shores of Britain. Despite this Patrick had set up his Church at Saul in south east Down, but Comgall had no plans to resurrect Patrick's achievement at Downpatrick. Comgall hunted the badger and it was eaten in Ulster until very recently. Many varieties of wild boar were trapped or killed with slings.

Comgall, unlike Francis of Assisi (thirteenth century), had no qualms about killing fowl, and this was in entire agreement with the Bible. The Gaels did not like heron flesh. Some have said that hunting was a sport rather than an economic necessity, but this ignores the conditions of society and the Church in the sixth century. All lands in North Down came under the influence of Comgall and it seems incredible that he did not rear livestock for use in the abbey.

Fishing in both the sea and land was of great importance. According to the laws and the annals great emphasis was laid upon fishing as a means of sustenance. Comgall and his monks sailed into the waters of the Irish Sea and Belfast Lough, casting their nets. Comgall must have been aware of the role of the apostles, who were called upon to become fishers of men. Perhaps Comgall expected to see a vision of Saint Peter, or see Christ walking upon the waters. Water played a great role in Catholic Christianity for were not men and infants baptized in it. The Red Sea parted its waters under command of God, so that the Israelites might pass, and so that Pharaoh's men would perish. God had destroyed the earth with water and had sent rainbows — He promised never to destroy life on earth again with water. Some Christian sects believe that water can be used in holy communion, for holy communion was only a symbolic act, taking the place of wine.

The River Bann flowed through central Ulster as well as the River Bush, both centres of Christianity in the north. The North Channel flanked the coast of County Antrim, and over these waters migrants and immigrants had passed setting up Irish kingdoms in Argyll, later to be known as Scottish Dalriada. In County Down there was Strangford Lough, later to be held by the Vikings, and further south lay Carlingford Lough, also of Viking origin. The economic importance of fish can be seen from the law tracts, but in the sixth century rights over fishing in certain areas was not yet commonplace. It was left to the Middle Ages to bring this about. Christ had said that he was a "fisher of men". The sign of the fish denoted faith in Christ. The Catholic Church in Italy had grown up near the waters of the Mediterranean, and it was from Ostia, the port of Rome, that many disciples left Rome to bring the Church to the many nations of Europe. They must also have made the inland journey, across the Alps and into France or Gaul. Some missionaries like that of Palladius and Patrick had made Eirinn their goal.

It is said that Saint Peter was Christ's favourite apostle, for had not Christ given to Peter "the keys of the kingdom of heaven", did he not mean that Peter should be the first Pope, baptizing in the name of the father, son and holy spirit.

In regard to Ulster there were severe penalties laid down for those who violated fishing rights and for interference with weirs. Fishing weirs, equally private and protected by the law, were erected in tidal waters and estuaries. Perhaps fishing rights were royal rights in the sixth century; certainly Comgall's Church took enthusiastically to real fishing and fishing for men. Fish had been important in the spread of civilization, in a world that knew nothing of potatoes or modern food conveniences. The Romans were great fishers in the Mediterranean or in Latin "Our Sea".

In an earlier chapter it was stated that the Romans may have tried to conquer Ireland, using Ulster as a base, with the short sea journey between the County Antrim coast and Kintyre in Western Scotland. Comgall would also travel to Lough Neagh and its plentiful waters for fishing. The Gaels were very much aware of the value of their inland waters. The fishermen of Lough Neagh complained to the saint that there was not enough fish to be caught. Sea fishing was probably carried out by currach. Shellfish, limpets, periwinkles, oysters and scapple were eaten. The East Down coast, the North Down coast and the coast of Antrim were all areas of plentiful supplies of fish. Today there are many little villages or townlands along the Down and Antrim coast from which the fishermen launch their boats for a catch.

The Antrim coast stretched from the shores of Belfast Lough, into the Larne area, then up the coast to Cushendun. From here the modern road probes inland until at last it reaches Portrush or Port Rosse. At Portrush there is a good view of Scotland.

Edible seaweeds were also of economic importance. Duilesc or dulse was a condiment of the legal diet of the commoner-farmer. Today along the Antrim coast dulse can be farmed, for example at the little port of Carnfunnock, just four miles out of Larne to the west, or a mile or so from the modern settlement of Ballygally. Dulse was also picked along the rest of the Antrim coast. The coast reaches the north west coast of County Londonderry. Here at Doire or Derry, Saint Comgall would have worshipped in the famous monastery there, Saint Columba's great foundation. The monks of Doire fished in the Atlantic Ocean, leading a similar life to the monks and brothers of Bangor Abbey. Both monasteries competed with one another in their worship of Christ and the Virgin Mary. Derry carried on close relations with Columba's other foundation at Iona in the Western Isles of Scotland.

From ancient times Derry was a stopping off point to the west of Scotland. Perhaps Comgall too took ship from Derry and travelled to see his old friend Columba or Columkille. Derry was the focus of life in the north west, its influence extending into the kingdom of Tirconnell or Donegal. Derry's monastic rule was accepted by many monasteries of the north coast of Ulster with Bangor's influence perhaps also spreading south into the kingdom of Biarrche or Mourne. Derry stood on the west bank of the River Foyle. From here Comgall sailed up the river to the present day Strabane region. All along this route the Donegal Mountains rose to the north and to the Sperrin Mountains in the east. There was plenty of timber in the Sperrin Mountains; timber for making wooden churches and chapels and for making currachs. The river was rich in fish. Looking out to the north east the great Foyle estuary shimmered, and from here ships sailed to Scotland and maybe further afield into lands far into the Atlantic Ocean.

In the North Down region stood the many ráiths, usually circular with a mean diameter of about one hundred feet, where stood the dwelling house and out offices. Farm buildings were also erected outside the periphery of the enclosure. Within the ráith there were also a variety of structures of difference materials, both free standing and lean to. It appears that the surrounding wall was the most important item. The buildings within the ráith were constructed with whatever material was available. Except for the larger castles, where the surrounding walls were made out of stone, the houses were also built of stone. Otherwise timber, clay, turf, and wattle and daub were used. Both dwelling houses and churches were made out of wood, but it is likely that stone was also used. However building in wood, according to the British historian Bede, was characteristic of the Gaels. According to one source Saint Brigit made a house of a hundred loads of peeled rods which she obtained under questionable circumstances from the King of Leinster. The turf or clay walls of a ráith was meant to keep out enemies. At Derry a good stone wall was a bulwark against various hostile tribes. Saint Kevin of Glendalough built himself a house made out of twigs, and this fashion may have been true of Comgall's Bangor. The walls of the monastery were there to keep the world out not to keep the monks in. The monasteries also had to be constructed so that bad weather could not destroy them. Lighter structures in the North Down area were prey to thunder and lightning and were blown away if the structures were made out of wood, so perhaps stone was a likely used material. There are references in the law tracts to the "dam liac" or stone house, usually a church, and certainly by AD 789 there was a stone rectory at Armagh.

It is likely that Bangor Abbey was built out of stone, in keeping with the monasteries at Glendalough in County Wicklow and Derry in County Londonderry. On the ordinary house, roofing was made out of thatch, and in those days no one had to await for planning permission! A site was chosen and a few friends would lend their help over a period of time. Most of the houses were probably built without any foundation. The rural thatching was one task which many men could do, but few could do well. A thatcher's skill could only be learned over a period of time. There was a resident thatcher in almost every townland, and it took a steady hand to be one. Thatchers working near the coast, as at Bangor in North Down, needed special skills, for the thatch had to withstand many storms.

Methods of thatching varied from place to place and to the materials used. A good thatcher took pride in his work. In coastal areas where the thatch had to be fashioned with ropes and weights, the thatch looked very attractive with its crisscross patters of ropes. The thatcher had his set of special tools, for example the yoke was used to either carry a burden of straw or to hold the straw in position beside the thatcher on the roof while he worked. The thatcher worked in all weathers, and he was aware that the thatch was highly inflammable, but in ancient Ulster it seldom caught fire.

The first reference to lead roofing is made in the annals of Ulster in 1009, but it may have existed at an earlier date. It is likely that parts of Bangor Abbey, namely its roofing, was made out of lead and other materials, as early as the sixth century. Metals were very dear to not only the monks but to the common man and the aristocracy. Outside of monastic walls, special houses were also built for large scale entertainments, weddings and other occasions. These structures may have existed at Emain Macha (Armagh) at the height of the kingdom of Ulster. Emain Macha was the headquarters of the Red Branch Knights, a sort of Ulster Round Table. At Emain Macha lead and other materials existed side-by-side with thatched buildings. The layout of a North Down house has to rest upon reconstruction, for there are very few records upon which we can rely. Reconstruction can take place by reading the law tracts. Sleeping quarters were not separate to the houses and huts. Beds were arranged about the walls, but in the houses of the rich some protection or form of cubicle may have surrounded the beds. Strewn straw or rushes, which were frequently changed, were used as general bedding. Ticks stuffed with straw, rushes and other materials, were used, mostly in the houses of the wealthy. Also the rich used beds with bedposts, made out of wood. Kings kept their swords and their valuables in such bedsteads. Rugs and skins, especially calf skins were used as bed covers. Paving was not possible in poor huts, and normally beds were shared. However visiting poets insisted on separate beds. Kings also shared their beds and the office of a king's bedfellow was an important position.

The duty of a royal poet was to lull the king to sleep. It was common practise to strew the floor of the house with rushes or with fresh straw. Skins covered the beds, especially calf skins and the hairier the better. Skins were also used for seats in carts and as rugs upon which people sat when indoors. Rudimentary stools and tables must have been in use, but there is no evidence of sophisticated furniture. The hearth or fire lay in the centre of the hut and the smoke escaped through vents and holes in the walls and roofs. The Gaels, as well as Comgall in his monastery, knelt in front of the fire, singing songs and having a drink or two. For Comgall heat was God's blessing, especially in the winter months.

Ulster was a very heavily wooded land, so perhaps buildings of wood came as second nature, and wood was an important domestic fuel. The region of North Down was no doubt covered in forests, and from these forests the Abbey of Bangor may have first been built, to be later built mostly of stone. However we learn from the law tracts that turf was the main fuel. To the south lay the Mountains of Mourne and their turf lands; to the north, across Belfast Lough, lay the Antrim plateau, also with its plentiful turf. Turf was used in Ulster from very earliest times to fuel fires in a land in which there were no great coal deposits. As a child and as a young man Comgall left Magheramourne, his birthplace, to travel into the Antrim plateau, to observe the turf cutters and to load up with turf himself for his mother and father — using a lot of turf if he was born into the upper classes, and using only a little turf if he had been born into the more servile people. The cutting, saving and carriage of turf required less labour and far less equipment than the cutting of wood. It is less likely to throw out sparks in the inflammable atmosphere of the thatched houses and huts.

Candles were also made by dipping rushes in tallow. Very large candles were used to light the interior of Bangor Abbey, along with the houses of the wealthy. Domestic vessels were seldom made out of metal, and wooden vessels were for popular use. Water for bathing at the abbey, and in the community, was heated by throwing hot stones into water. Similar methods were used to stew meat, both indoors and outdoors. An aigen, a cooking vessel or pan, was used for baking and possibly for other cooking purposes. In the law tracts we learn that a spoon was a sort of cooking pan. Wooden vessels and platters were made of elder, oak and other woods. Large hoop-bound staves were used to build vessels of high quality as churns and containers for milk, or other bulk liquids. The monks of the abbey set to work like the peasants; spinning, weaving, basket making and producing domestic items of wood and leather. The monks may also have made weapons for sale to the aristocracy and warrior classes, despite the biblical strictures about violence and killing.

The monks welcomed visitors and the poor within its walls. The spirit of hospitality was widely valued. Washing and bathing are referred to continually, but the level of personal hygiene was much to be desired.

Both lords and commoners lived in poor conditions in comparison with modern times. The chief amusements of the upper classes were music, storytelling, board games and drinking. Wine was imported directly from the Atlantic ports of Gaul or France. Ale was by far the most popular drink in the small houses and at the abbey. Wine remained an aristocratic drink. The law tracts detail the manufacture of ale and it had to be made to the highest standards. It was also used to pay rents and discharge legal debts. Ale was forbidden in stricter monastic circles like that the Céli Dé, except when the monks went on long journeys.

Chapter 14

Another Look at the Gaels.

It has been seen how Ptolemy described the geographical, cultural and historical state of Ireland around AD 84. Following or during this period the Lagin people invaded the modern Leinster, and the Damnoni invaded from south western Scotland under pressure from the Roman Empire. Soon Ireland was divided into four parts or provinces. There was the Iverni now known as Munster, the Lagin of Leinster, the Uluti (Ulaid), Ulster and the Ol Nechnacht, now known as Connaught. It appears that Ulster looked larger than the other kingdoms, and was the most important Gaelic state. Ptolemy enumerates the tribes that inhabited the coast of Ireland and its interior. On the northern coast dwelt the Vennicnii, in the modern county of Donegal, and the Robogdi in Derry and Antrim. Adjoining to the Vennicnii westward lay the lands of the Eradi or Erpeditarii, and next to them the Nagnatae, all in Donegal. The Nagnatae also occupied North Connaught. Further were the Auterii (the Uaithni) in Sligo and Galway, the Gangani in Mayo and the Velliborii in the lands between the Shannon and Galway. The whole of the north west part of Ireland with a large part of the interior was occupied by the Iverni; the name derives from Ierne or "Ireland", and has not been proven of Gaelic origin, although it was used in everyday speech as "Ireland" and "Eirinn". The Celts were the first Europeans north of the Alps to emerge into recorded history in Ulster.

The first reference to them dates back to the sixth century BC. They confronted other European nations and tribes, and when they emerge into history in Ulster they are known as the Keltoi by the Greeks not only in Ulster but in Europe generally. Polybius also uses the word "Galetae" which by his time became widely used by the Greeks. Diodorus Siculus (c.60-30 BC) considered that the term "Celt" was the proper name for the people he was describing. Pansariius (AD c.160) gives priority to the name Celt over the names "Gauls" or "Galatians". Julius Caesar remarked (100 — 44 BC) that the Gauls of his time referred to themselves as Celtae.

In Ulster this must also have been the case, and Comgall regarded himself as a Celt or Gael, a descendant of the Celtic tribes that reached Ireland/ Ulster. It is almost certain that the word "Keltoi" or Celt, was a word of Celtic origin. It is not clear what the meaning of the word is; the Irish from of the word is "ceilt", meaning concealment or secret; and has given us the word "Kilt".

The Gaels did not write down their history, and this may be one of the reasons why the Celts were regarded as "the secret people". The Gaels, under Comgall, took a religious view and prohibited the writing down of history for the sake of the kingdom of God. Throughout Europe there were several versions of the Celtic language, and Gaelic in Ulster was only one of them. Historians and archaeologists are agreed that the start of the Iron Age in Europe saw the Celts expand in Europe, identified with the Hallstartt culture, using a cradle in the Alps as an expanding point, but the arrival of the Gaels in Ulster may date back to 1000 BC. It seems likely that there were Celts in Europe and Ulster by 700 BC. Iron objects have been classified at their points of distribution at La Tene, giving its name to another variety of Celts.

The Celtic language dates back to a time when most of the European languages shared a common root. The Gaels in Ulster share this common heritage. These languages were known as "Indo-European", and existed in origin sometime before the rise of the Roman Republic. The languages broke up into families of Latin, Slavic, German, Celtic and so forth. Before 200 BC it is true to say that Celtic was evolving into a language. Comgall, as well as speaking Latin, presumably was fluent in Gaelic. It is not clear whether mass was said in the vernacular or in Latin. Latin has a long tradition in the Catholic Church, and the disciples and apostles of Christ may have had knowledge of the language as well as their day to day Hebrew. The Celts however in Europe were never able to unite themselves into an empire, although the term "Celtic Empire" has been used to describe Celtic civilization. There was nothing new in Ulster about Celtic civilization, and most of Ulster's history is based upon traditions. The Romans, it is said, never reached Eirinn, apart from trading expeditions, probably on the east coast of the island, with its picturesque ports.

It is thought that the Celts may have spoken a common European language and had accepted the rise of political Rome. As the political system developed, the language broke into several versions, so that today we have the Gaelic spoken in Ulster and the rest of Ireland. Scholars think that this universal Celtic was spoken just before the start of the first millennium BC. After this two different languages may have emerged — Goidelic and Brythonic. The famous Welsh, Cornish and Breton were also included. The Romans did not succeed in completely destroying the Celts and their languages, but Latin of course was thought to be superior.

The Celts had no common European capital, although they can be termed as a civilization or a culture. The Celts had regional capitals like that of Emain Macha in Ulster (at Armagh) and Cashel in the province of Munster. Children at North Down and adults at Bangor Abbey were brought up to speak Gaelic, but they may also have had a knowledge of Latin. It is not known how proficient Comgall was in this dead language; presumably he was on a par with his great friend and missionary, Saint Columba of Derry or Iona. Also, it is not known if there were dialects of Gaelic spoken in Ulster and the Western Isles of Scotland. The historian assumes that one dialect prevailed, but that there was in the early years, a divided Ulster, divided culturally and politically.

Where did the Celts in Ulster develop their distinctive culture? Undoubtedly they brought their culture and language with them from that cradle in the Alps. Presumably at one time the Romans felt themselves under threat from such a warlike people. The Celts of Europe must have brought their gods with them, to be replaced at a later date by Christianity. The Celts did not think that their power in Europe would be overthrown, nor indeed in Ulster that the Gaels would be subjected by the Normans. Christ had saving power but society looked down at the liberalism of the Church. This was a land that had been troubled by wars from an early date, long before the Gaels arrived at Emain Macha or before the foundation of the Ulster monasteries. Comgall may not have regarded himself as an Ulsterman but only an inhabitant of a local kingdom based in the North Down region. To him, there were many powers in Ulster — the power of the Rí at Armagh, the power of the druids — and the power of the Church. Comgall feared ancient paganism and he ever sought to evangelize the bleaker aspects of Gaelic society in the kingdom of the Ulaid (mostly covering present day Ulster or the Six Counties).

Before all else Comgall believed in the saving power of the Church, a Church he had believed in for many years before he established himself at Bangor. As a Gael he became famous in Ireland in his lifetime, following in the footsteps of Patrick, Columba and Columbanus. He must have regarded both Latin and Gaelic as religiously inspired languages of Church and people.

The institution of monasticism is not mentioned in the Bible. The origins of monasticism may date back to the second century onwards. The monastery became the centre of culture, civilization and mission. The Western world had a number of religious orders that flourished in Dark Age Europe. The Celtic and Benedictine forms emerged and had existed side by side throughout most of Europe and in those troubled times monasticism was to become the centre of religious activity in the West, as Bangor Abbey and the other institutions spread their influence by the sixth century.

With the edict of Milan, legalizing Christianity in AD 313, large numbers started to join the Church. These monasteries in Europe were to become very worldly bodies, but Bangor and the other Ulster monasteries kept matters plain and fundamental as a measure of faith. From very earliest times the Church in general came across unmarried and celibate women. Often this meant that the Church supported the efforts of women, some of whom founded monasteries of their own. At times of persecution the nuns as well as the monks would live their lives for the sake of the kingdom of God. With the edict of Milan the newly converted were not called upon to be martyrs.

As an emotional Gael Comgall welcomed the role of women in his Church. Men and women were equal in the eyes of God, and was not the Virgin Mary the mother of Jesus? The first monk in Ulster, as elsewhere, looked back upon the gradual rise of monasticism within the Gaelic Church. By the sixth century Bangor had been well established and could look forward to a long period of prosperity in Ulster despite the arrival of the Danes. At Bangor the Gaelic monks congregated together for worship and celebration of the eucharist on Saturdays and Sundays.

The first monastic establishment of monasticism in Europe was that of Martin of Tours, established at Poitiers. The establishment of monasticism not only in Europe, but in Ulster, brought changes to society. Whilst Christianity had been well established in the duns, raths and forts, the farms and countryside were perhaps mainly pagan. Preaching missions into the Ulster countryside were high on Comgall's agenda. The example of Martin of Tours was followed closely in Ulster. Comgall believed that the monk and abbot, rather than the priest and bishops were more capable of bringing to the countryside the word of God. Clearly Bangor acted as a support for the rís or kings rather than as representing a threat. The pagan kings became Christian and presumably remained Christian. Comgall relied upon royal patronage for land and some times for protection. Many of the early saints were the sons of kings. The royal monks were at ease with the other monks in Ulster.

The monks fulfilled the role of druid, Brehon or bard. Bangor and its sister houses attracted a large number of monks, but perhaps monasticism in Ulster in the age of Saint Comgall was in large part an upper class and aristocratic organization. The Gaels had in common methods of warfare known to the European Celts, and the Ulster annals and other historians bear witness to this. The basic political division in sixth century Ireland can be traced back to the provinces and kingdoms that made up ancient Eirinn, Ulster, Leinster, Munster and Connaught. Ulster had her enemies, for example the province of Connaught or Connacht. From the Tain we learn that the three warrior septs of Ireland were the Ganuuraid (Domnainn) from Irris Domnann, the Clan Dedad of Munster (Eirinn) and the Ulaid (Ulster). These tribes are pre Gaelic but important to the history of Ulster. From these tribes arose the Gaelic "nation", the earliest known Irish Gaelic is inscribed on the Ogham stones. The Ogham alphabet is based on the Latin one and is typified by a system of dots and strokes. Ogham seems to have been introduced into Ulster via the vassal tribes of Deisi, who had settled in western Britain but who have left evidence of these tribes in Munster. They also denote, for the first time, the superiority of Gaelic speech. The Gaels proper (Feni) have sometimes been mistaken with other Gaelic speaking vassals.

The Gaels from the outset were a violent people, and as a Gael Comgall was aware of his ancestor's warlike nature. The then history of Ulster was Gaelic inspired in its earliest state. There was no writing down of the genealogies and histories. The original peoples of Ulster were mostly confined now (sixth century) to the area comprised of the present day counties of Antrim and Down. In Gaelic the kingdom was known as Ulaid or the Latin Ulidia. So long as the Gaelic kingdom of Ulster was divided, the Uí Neill could not proclaim themselves as Kings of Ulster. The independent territories became known by their Gaelic names (Dál meaning "part of"). Of the Ulster kingdoms there remained only the Dál Fitach of County Down, whilst their northern kinsmen were known as the Dál Riada or the people of Riada, their lands becoming known as the kingdom of Dalriada. The Ulaid remained in possession of the maritime ports of County Down. It is thought that the many people of Antrim and Down were of the ancient kindred of Cruithin. The Manapi (Fermanagh) and their kinsmen were known as the Brigantes (Ui Bairche) who dwelled mostly in the Mourne Mountains of South Down, where they had been driven by the Lagin. A remnant of the Fermanagh tribes remained along the shores of Lough Erne.

It was the Cruithin that made up most of the population of old Ulidia. The ancient kindred covered mostly the present day counties of Antrim and Down, and the area from Lough Foyle to Dundalk bay. The name of the main dynasty was Dál n Araidi and the state that they founded became known as Dalriada in English. There may have existed about seven to nine petty Dalaradian kingdoms in the sixth century. North west of the Lower River Bann dwelt the Cruithin of Arda Eolaig and the Li. The northern Dál n Araidi extended from Lough Neagh northwards to the Atlantic and North Channel, and included Coleraine and its environs, which are now County Londonderry. In County Down the southern kindred (Hí Echach Cobhan) inhabited the present day baronies of the Upper and Lower Iveagh and Kilalarty. The boundary between the kingdom of Oriel and Ulster was marked by an earthen wall, known as "The Dane's Court" and it can be seen to this day. It runs from Scarva in Down to Meigh, not far from Killeavy, and Slieve Gullion in County Armagh. The earthen wall consists of a wide fosse or trench with a rampart on either side. Part of the wall was heavily mounted, bearing witness to the expanding population of the region. The main fortifications were at Listullyard. Parts of the wall command the Moiry Pass. The purpose of the wall was to remain important for two hundred years. The midland Gaels expanded into Ulster, and the destruction of the province's power was to change the course of history in ancient Ulster. The Ulster Scotti invaders landed a series of attacks against the Scots of the Western Isles. The Scottish colonies were to overshadow the power of the Antrim Scots and it eventually went its own way. The sixth century was an important century for the development of the Gaelic language. There was a widespread adoption of Gaelic speech by the original inhabitants and there were Brittonic loan words into Gaelic. The Scots of the two Dalriada kingdoms (Antrim and Argyll) regarded themselves as Gaels. At this point the Cruithin preserved their own Gaelic origins, but Gaelic became the accepted tongue. As a result of the warlike activities of the Uí Neill, and inland trouble, the Cruithin and Ulaid went into further decline in Ireland, and the focus of their activities centred in northern Britain. AD 562 was an important year; one entry in the annals of Ulster records that there were several important battles in the north of Ireland. The opposing armies were led, on one side, by "seven kings of the Cruithin in alliance with the northern Uí Neill". The Celtic (Gaelic) tribes varied in size, some comprising an entire "nation", as in Ulaid and other tribal regions.

The Uí Neill was of course the most important "national" unit based at Ailech in present day County Donegal. In Europe some tribes and national units could reach 390,000 strong. The Gaels looked after their sick, and hospitals had been established in Ulster before the sixth century. The "hospital" is a phenomenon of pre-Christian Ireland, and it was taken over by the Catholic Church, which distributed alms. To understand the history of the Gaels of Ulster, it is useful to study them in relation to the history of Eirinn of Ireland. Celtic religion was the first to develop the idea of immortality. The Celts were familiar to both the Greek and Romans, upon whom we rely for facts. Death, so Comgall learned, as far as the Gaels were concerned, was a changing state and life went on in the next world, very much like life before birth. There was the fabulous underworld, and souls could be reborn into the present world.

The Gaels celebrated birth with mourning and death with joy. This was very much like the Christian view of mankind. The Gaels of North Down could rush into battle with the assurance of a life after death. Comgall taught that it was necessary to lead a good life if there was to be a life after death. The concept of Heaven is obscure and the pagan religions seem to be more definite about the afterlife as well as rewards in this life in exchange for good works. In many pagan religions fond objects were buried with a person, usually of the ruling classes. Egyptian civilization has Pharaoh pictured with his favourite servants buried with him. Christianity introduced ordinary methods of burial but the Gaels believed in cremation. The Christian hereafter attracted Gaels to Comgall's God, for a person might achieve a state of nirvana, and be perpetually united with Jesus Christ and his mother. Most religions have preached that death was not the end of life. Comgall proceeded to perform good works, so that his place in Heaven would be assured.

Chapter 15

The Celtic Supernatural

The Gaels of Ulster and Ireland were obsessed with magic and ritual, and were prime targets for the ritualistic Church of Rome. They were obsessed much more than the average European Celt about their religion. However the Gaels did not regard themselves as a religious people. As with other superstitious people the Gaels believed that magical agencies and powers pervaded their lives. The unseen powers were to be understood by the Gaelic people and their warriors. They recited myths, and these tales were used for moral ends. However in contrast to the Roman system, the Gaels had no defined pantheon, but the Armagh gods had their place in Gaelic beliefs. Despite destruction by the Church, there are quite a number of pagan histories that have come down to us. We learn that there were numerous deities. The pagan year was divided into warm and cold. In Ulster these seasons were divided into four festivals. In North Down Comgall celebrated along with the small number of pagans the great festival of Samain, and this was celebrated on the first of November, but the night preceding Samain was also important. Samain marked the end of one year and the beginning of a new year. Its position also stood independently between the two and it is pasturalist rather than an agrarian cycle.

The build up to the Christian New Year started on 25th December when Christ's birth was celebrated and when Comgall condemned the pagan gods. It was cold at Bangor Abbey and the monks sat around fires talking about their religion, and looking up to their abbot. The Celtic New Year coincided with the end of the grazing season. Under primitive conditions, the herds and flocks were brought together, and those animals required for breeding were spared from slaughter. This was a practise that dated back into Celtic tradition, with the Neolithic farmers. The word Samain seems to be best interpreted as meaning a reassembly or gathering together and in Ulster the tuatha may be envisaged as reuniting at an

Óenach at this time. The festival of Samain inspired the North Down warriors as they looked up to Comgall's Gaelic Church. Sacrifices were offered up at this festival, but no material descriptions have survived. The earth was renewed, both to gods and warriors and for Christians. The god Dagda enters the scene with a goddess, the Morrígan, or in another instance, with Boann, the deity of the River Boyne, geographically in the north of Ireland. "Dagda" means the good god, but not good in the ethical sense, but good at everything or all competent. Dagda is the father of the tribe, its protector and benefactor, and this is true of all pagan deities in Ulster in the sixth century. There was no such exclusive deity for war, they were all manifestations of the tribal god. Dagda had a mate and she was a nature goddess, one Morrígan, Queen of Demons, and she appears frequently in the Irish texts. His name was interchangeable with other horrific demons such as Nemain (Panic) and Badb Catha (Raven of Battle). There were other goddesses, namely Macha and Medb (Maeve) that introduced great changes. These gods and goddesses, displaying both fertility and destructive aspects, may be symbolized by way of the Sun and Moon. On the eve of Samain the Celtic world was supposed to be overrun by magical qualities. Magical troops issued from caves and mounds; men might be admitted into the circle of the gods whilst royal fortresses (and monasteries) might be attacked by the prevailing demons.

The second most important festival in Ulster in the sixth century was the feast of the first of May, the start of the warm season; it was called Beltane of Cetshamain, i.e., it was a predominantly pastoral festival, when the cattle were driven into the open fields for grazing. Great fires were lit, a practise that lasted beyond the sixth century. The cattle would be driven between fires to protest against any sort of magic, and this practise was overseen by the druids. The word "Beltane", incorporating the Gaelic word for fire, is probably to be connected with the Latin god Beleuus, which appears to be the oldest Gaelic god, associated principally with pastoral activities.

The other two important festivals in Ulster were Lugnasad on the 1st of August and the festival of Imbolc of which we know very little. Imbolc has been associated as marking the beginning of the lactation of ewes, and it corresponds with the feast of Saint Brigit in the Christian calendar. In pagan times Brigit was a wise woman and daughter of the Dagda. She was an important fertility goddess. She had the powers of learning and healing. The pagan Brigit can be traced back into Celtic European history as being the exalted one. Imbolc has since pagan times been associated with the keeping of sheep, but this animal possessed no ritual status like the ox, the boar and the dog. It is not known when these festivals were incorporated into Christianity or condemned by it, as is also the case of the last festival of Lugnasad, probably introduced into Ulster quite late on. The festival is entirely agrarian, which reflected not only the other provinces in Ireland, but also Ulster in particular. The festival presided over the ripening of the crops, and observances were kept pagan style for the forthcoming harvest. The god Lug appears later in the history of the Ulster gods; he is a tribal god. His name of course is well known in Lugudunum, the modern Lyons in France, and a number of other European names. At this festival Lug was also worshipped by a female deity and this can be traced to the ancient god Macha of Armagh in central Ulster.

Perhaps Lug was brought to Ulster by Gaulish settlers in the first century BC. There was another name for the August festival, Brun Trograin. Sacrifices were offered up on its feast day. The calendar from which these feasts were celebrated was mentioned in both Irish and classical sources. These seem to be based on lunar observations and to have been counted in nights rather than days. It is thought that the actual choice of day lay in the hands of the druids, who would have decided the importance of some of the days. The success of a tribe was also considered dependent upon religious ritual and the success of the rí. This matter is well documented in the texts. The failure of crops, cattle disease or other misfortunes might be attributed to the unsuitability of a rí.

The Gaelic kings of North Down and southern Antrim were thought as being the descendants of the territorial nature gods and goddesses. There is however no evidence to show that the rís were divine, in the same way the Roman emperors were considered to be divine. The king possessed a mortal wife, and of course the king himself had to grow old.

Comgall's monastic system had to grow old with its abbot and monks, who would all go to Heaven for leading a good life. The Gaelic kings in pagan times, meet with a violent end, and there are a number alluded to by wounding, drowning and burning in the midst of high magic, in the presence of the tribal gods. In the stories associated with Samain, the Dagda is represented by a grotesque figure of immense strength and appetite. He is clad in a short garment of a servant; his weapon is a great club, sometimes dragged on wheels and he possesses a magical cauldron, which has inexhaustible qualities. The symbol of abundance in Ulster is represented by a number of mythological stories. By contrast Lug is often portrayed as a young man of a much less primitive concept, showing more of the bleaker sides to the Dagda. As far as animals are concerned the horse played some sort of role in Gaelic society, continuing long after the sixth century. The horse is known by a variety of mythological names such as Eochaid, the Ro-Each, the latter meaning the "great horse". Horse symbolism is closely attached to the goddesses, and the most widespread name is Epona, a goddess sometimes featured by Gallo-Roman authors.

Another important Gaelic deity, male and female, is that of Tripalism, a matter which has been explored a great deal, but it is thought that it has no importance as far as the teaching of the Trinity is concerned. The number "three" is important when discussing ancient people — Saint Patrick is said to have preached the concept of the Trinity by using a three leaf shamrock in his sermons to the Gaels. Comgall may have followed in the footsteps of Patrick.

The deities could be of either sex, and there is a more pronounced attitude amongst the goddesses and of three different names, as in Morrígan, Badl, Nenian, who was the equivalent of Morrígan in the plural; there are three Brigits and three Machas. The triad are three Brigits, Eire, Banba, and Fodla may be less ancient although the individual names can claim genuine antiquity. Of others, both Carmen and Tlachlga gave birth to triplate sons, reminding us once again of the role of the number "three" in religions. This triad amongst the monasteries takes various forms. However principle characters such as the Dagda and Lug are not strongly triple, although the Dagda had ascribed to him two other names, and Lug had two brothers and arrived at Tara with two companions. The early years in Christian Ulster are marked by the crumbling away of the pagan deities and the Christian monasteries taking over. There is evidence to show that North Down was a federation of tribes, within which Bangor Abbey operated. Tradition has stated that Saint Patrick reformed the Brehon laws in the fifth century, but he failed to change the Gaelic laws on marriage, illegitimacy, divorce and polygamy. This was the state of affairs Saint Comgall was left with. He was unable to let the Irish clergy practise celibacy. The Gaels lived within the old laws until the sixteenth century. During the sixth century in Ulster life expectance was only twenty-four years, and staying alive for a long time was a great achievement.

The laws in force in the sixth century took a realistic approach to life. The Gaels had no jails. As far as society was concerned, men were more equal than women. The early Gaelic laws disapproved of "one night stands" and prostitution. Indeed a prostitute's son, evocatively called "son of the bushes" was effectively disinherited since no one could ever be sure who his father was. Abortion was illegal. A man could divorce his wife who induced or obtained an abortion (the Brehon laws suggested that abortion was caused by a woman refusing to eat). Saint Patrick seems to have accepted married clergy, and Comgall may have followed suit. Life of course was highly regulated within the walls of Bangor Abbey. Comgall, like the later Columbanus, forbade monks to wash alone if naked. The monks were obliged to hop into a common bath, and also to sit down so that the water covered their bodies. If a monk lifted a knee or an arm out of the water, he was penalized for flaunting himself, if the water was not strictly for washing. His punishment was that he was not allowed to wash again for another week.

Royal assembly places like Emain Macha (Armagh) were earthworks, like Tara, north of Dublin. At all of these there are earthworks with the ditch inside the rampart. The earthen works were usually a ritual device, and it was effective for defence if the earthworks were usually sited on sloping ground. In Ulster the juxtaposition, at the principle places of assembly of various kinds of enclosure with burial mounds stresses the importance of family burial tombs. The Gaels of Ulster therefore had their burial tombs and chambers. The rí or king could look forward to a happy life after death and all his prize possessions were buried with him. At the turn of the third century the power and resources of the Gaels of Ulster were viewed as quite formidable. It seemed a foregone conclusion that the Gaels would unite with the other clans in Ireland to form a single power in the island like the Roman imperial system. Fate dictated that the Gaelic and Celtic civilization would pass through a sharp decline. Distance in Ireland and in Europe spelt decline, for the Celtic highways were not as complex as the Roman ones. In Ulster the Gaels may have been ineffective warrior people, lacking the warlike attitudes of the Romans on the Continent. In Ulster, if given time the Gaels may have united into conquering Tara and setting up an Irish Empire, which had been talked about considerably in military and political circles.

The Gaels therefore lacked the political genius of Rome; perhaps they might have developed these skills over a long period of time, but this is a matter for speculation. There was pressure on the Celts from all sides. In the north lived the Germans, in the east the Dacians, and in the south the Romans. The third century marked a decline in Celtic influence in Europe and a similar decline in Ulster long before the arrival of the Church. By the sixth century only a fragment remained of Celtic influence in Europe, but in Eirinn this power seems to have lingered on to be conquered by the Christian kings and princes. The professional class safeguarded the traditions of the Celts. In the sixth century there seem to be three classes in society; the druids, the bards and between them an order that is variously known by a Gaulish or Frankish turn of terminology connected with the Latin (vates).

The druids had the highest social status — we have seen the influence of their great prophets and magicians. They officiated at sacrifices, made and enforced legal decisions and conducted their own elaborate system of education. The vates are generally represented as expert in divination, but some think that they do not earn the title of a different class owing to their magical powers. They may have been subordinate druids. Literature and its understanding was left to the bards, and history has described them as singers of praise. The accuracy of these facts is attested by reference in the Ulster annals and other documents.

In the classical authors we also run up against three classes in Ulster — the druid (druidh), filidh and bards (baird). As in Europe it was difficult to discuss the difference in some of the orders. The filidh eventually helped to carry out the role of the druids in Ulster, also common to other European Celts. The filidh established themselves and they eventually carried on the role of the druids by the sixth century. They also established relations with Bangor Abbey and other Ulster/Irish religious establishments. The filidh were something more important than poets. They were seers, teachers, advisers to rulers, witnesses to contracts. By the seventeenth century the order was eventually disbanded with pressure coming from the English government. As poets they trampled into territory that was allotted to the bards (baird). The Irish bards were once closely associated with the composition of praise-poetry, like their counterparts in Gaul. The filidh however expanded their sphere of influence replacing the druids as founts of knowledge and poetry. The bards that made their way to Bangor Abbey are represented as being of second rate importance. In Ulster the curriculum of the student filidh extended over a period of at least seven years. The Gaelic druids elected a leader of their own, also a practise of the filidh. The earliest sources for the history of the Celts in Europe give us some information how tribal "status" in the Celtic Empire was run. The historical tales made up an important part of the filidh's repertoire, and many of these are concerned with the supernatural world and for that reason modern scholars sometimes refer to the mythological cycle. Most of the Irish tales are mythological to a greater or lesser extent. There is much to be said of the native system of classification which groups individual titles not by cycle but by theme; plundering, cattle raids, wooings, battles, voyages, adventures, elopements, etc. The remaining tales can be divided into three broad categories; miscellaneous tales assigned to the various kings, historic and prehistoric, the cycle of the Ulaidh or "Ulstermen" with Conor Mac Nessa their king and Cu Chulainn their youthful hero. Finally there is the cycle of Finn Mac Cumhaill and the roving bands of warriors called the Fianna.

The Ulster cycle was the most important document for the early period and it concerns itself with the activities and virtues that typify other heroic cultures and states. There is also the Fionn cycle which was more important amongst the lower levels of society and less highly esteemed by the filidh. The chief occupation of the Fianna was hunting and lends colour to the annals and cycles. There is also the pseudo-historical works and particularly the Leabhar Gabhala, the Book of Invasions, and the Dinnshenchas, the history of places, all twelfth century works, but looking back upon Ulster's great past. The tales provide unity with diversity, and tell of the history of Ulster in the age of Saint Comgall.

Chapter 16

How Comgall Read the Gospels

Comgall believed in the Incarnation, for Jesus became man and dwelt amongst us. He fulfilled the words of the Old Testament, and gave to Peter the task of organizing the worldly Church at Rome; "The word became flesh" *(John 1:14)*. The story of Jesus, so Comgall learned from the gospels, took place in first century Palestine, a small country on the eastern shores of the Mediterranean. It is likely that the saint regarded the first four gospels as the work of the second half of the first century, produced somewhere within the bounds of the Roman Empire. The young Jesus and the infant Church grew up in the small country of Israel, situated between the Mediterranean and the Jordan river.

Jerusalem was both the capital of Judea and centre of the Jewish faith. Jesus's early ministry was centred upon Galilee. He was put to death in Jerusalem after quite a short ministry. For Comgall the crucifixion of Christ was the central act in Christianity and he searched for the meaning of the crucifixion as he preached to the tribes of North Down. Comgall's imagination was activated as he contemplated the Jerusalem temple, the covenant between God and the people of Israel. Jews who lived outside the Diaspora or agreement, were said to be dispersed, a Greek word meaning "scattering" or "dispersion".

There were a number of sects within Judaism — the Pharisees, Sadducees, Essenes, Samaritans, Zealots and Christians. The major Jewish centres were at Alexandria in Egypt, Antioch in Syria, and Rome. The Jews competed for power long after the collapse of Rome.

Comgall like all great saints, loved the gospels, for in the gospels was recorded the history of mankind. In the gospels God had written what he wanted the people of Ulster to do. The gospels told of the events that did not take place as everyday experience, for in the gospels were many miracles, for example the raising of Lazarus from the dead, the resurrection of Christ, and the Virgin birth. Comgall realized that he must believe in the gospels in order to go to Heaven. For Comgall Jesus existed not only as a person, but incorporated all aspects of the divine. Comgall's career centred around his search for the historical Jesus. There were Ulstermen who did not believe in the gospels, probably the druids to begin with, but with the help of men like Comgall, Jesus the "god" was presented to the Irish race. Many have claimed to hear the voice of Jesus, and Comgall accepted one hundred per cent the role of miracles within the Catholic Church.

The early years after the Church saw the recording of many miracles. It was up to the Papacy whether an evangelist should be canonized. Jesus in history spoke to the Gaels of Ulster. His gospel was for all mankind, for all of Ireland, a useful point to make in the political and religious history of Ulster today.

It is useful to look back at Jesus's mission; he proclaimed the coming of the kingdom of God, and his mission would start immediately within his lifetime. God was not only his creator but also his father. He proclaimed the forgiveness of sins and believed in the life everlasting. It was necessary, Comgall believed, to do good works if he wanted to take up one's place in the life everlasting. The first century was a period of great change in Rome, for it saw the transition between Republic and Empire. However the pagans were reigning and it seemed impossible that an obscure religion like that of Christianity should take up its place in the Roman pantheon. Comgall was taught from the gospels that he should love his enemy, for Christ had exhorted his followers to do good to those that despise you. It was a faith that never left Comgall, but he may have had his moments of doubt, though not perhaps like doubting Thomas. Comgall, through Christ's teaching, learnt to care for a variety of peoples — lepers, the sick, the lame, the poor, women, tax collectors and sinners. Perhaps the gospel according to Saint Luke was the gospel most dear to him. It is said that it was the most beautiful book ever written. The early Christians presented a considerable threat to the Jews, so the extent of Christian belief in the Empire was considerable. The chief sources for the life of Jesus are the four gospels, which carefully record the acts and miracles of the Messiah.

The first gospels are called the Synoptic Gospels. John is different and often had an independent view of Jesus; the outline, literary style and theology are different to Matthew, Luke and Mark. The Synoptic Gospels record Jesus's association with John the Baptist, his ministry of teaching and healing in Galilee, his journey to Jerusalem, his brief activity and teaching in the holy city, his passion (arrest, trial, death) and the discovery of the empty tomb. Jesus is referred to in various names — Son of Man, Son of David, Messiah, Son of God. The way the Synoptic Gospels record the life of Christ is called the Synoptic problem. These gospels record Christ's life and ministry from perhaps common sources. However there are striking differences. They address different audiences. These communities were under different pressures; Jewish Christians, persecution (Mark), and tension between rich and poor (Luke). They present different perspectives of Jesus; fulfilment of the Scriptures (Matthew), the suffering of the son of man and the prophet for example (Luke). They portray the disciples in different ways; there are men of little faith (Matthew), the cowardly (Mark) and the relationship of Christ within the Church (Luke).

Life within the Church must be studied, but let us take a look at the gospels and how Comgall regarded them with Christ and the Virgin Mary.

Unlike the letters of Paul or the Revelation, the gospel writers identify themselves. They may have regarded identifying as an act of friendship and faith with their flock. We learn that there were good men according to Matthew, Mark, Luke and John. There is a school of thought that states that the four gospels are amongst authors named as acts of piety. Rome is associated with the gospel writings, for as we have seen there were many persecutions of Christians in the first and second centuries. Perhaps Comgall loved the gospel of Mark, and its revolutionary atmosphere perhaps common to the other gospels and to the letters of Paul.

In recent years some schools of thought have placed the writings of Mark to Galilee and associated with them the destruction of the Jerusalem temple in AD 70. The gospel of Mark, like the other gospels, is based upon other Church traditions. Mark has come down to us as having great faith. Comgall, like Mark, loved the resurrection and sayings related to Jesus. There are no written records upon which Mark may have composed his gospel. The Church makes us believe that it was Mark, the disciple, that was inspired by the life of Christ and that he was the author of the text, a fundamentalist document. Above all Comgall viewed the spectacle of Christ on the Cross. Mark told the story of Christ as he bore witness during Christ's stay on earth. The first part of Christ's ministry takes place in Galilee. In the first part Jesus called together the first disciples and he had the ability to cure illness and to teach great wisdom. In the second part of Mark, Jesus deals with rejection, and he speaks in parables; "Blessed are those who are poor, for they shall see God. Blessed are those that mourn and search after righteousness for they shall be filled. Blessed are they that teach the word". Comgall was sure that he was one of the elect and that he would come face to face with the risen Christ in Heaven along with his mother, the Blessed Virgin Mary who had been taken up or assumed into Heaven, for she had great faith in her son. In the third part of Luke, Jesus begins by sending out his disciples to share in his mission, and ends with Mark's inability to understand the divine. Mark tells the story of John the Baptist, but he did not tell of John baptizing the missionary Christ. John's death is symbolic, for it predicts Christ's crucifixion. Mark tells the story of Christ's journey to Jerusalem and on the way he instructs the disciples in regard to his identity (Christology) and what it meant to follow him. Mark tells the story of a man that received his sight back as a result of fervent belief in Jesus.

Passion Week in Jerusalem is also mentioned. Jesus enters the city of Jerusalem and its temple area and offers prophetic teachings. He enters into a debate with his opponents. He tells the disciples what will happen in the future. The Passion tells of Jesus's anointing for death, the Last Supper, his prayer and arrest, his trials before the Jewish high priest and his trial before Pontius Pilate. At length he is crucified and there is the phenomenon of the empty tomb. The risen Christ had appeared before many people, taking place in the first and second centuries. In Mark memorable characters are recorded. The main character was Jesus of Nazareth, and Mark lets us know from the beginning that Jesus was the son of God. Jesus is portrayed as a wise teacher, an important belief for Comgall and his Christian God and converts. He is also portrayed as a powerful healer. Comgall understands that the true nature of Christ takes place upon his death. The centurion confessed that truly Jesus was the son of God.

Comgall read in the Scriptures that the mission of Christ was "to give life as ransom for many" and this Comgall believed in accordance with God's will. The disciples had eagerly followed this God of Gods; they realized that they too might have to be crucified by the Roman state and there were many prepared to die for Jesus and his claim that he was the son of God. Comgall was, like the disciples, ready to follow Christ immediately about hearing of the word. They would be called to heal the sick; their lives would be put at risk by contacting lepers. However Comgall learnt that he understood more about Christ as he read the gospels. His friendship with Christ progressed. During the ministry in Galilee Jesus asks them, "Do you still not understand?" Comgall at first, like all Christians, could not understand his vocation or calling to the Cross, and like the disciples he felt like deserting Christ when their faith was tested, or as in the New Testament, by persecution for the sake of their faith. Peter, the future Pope, denied Christ three times.

During his ministry Jesus met a variety of enemies and opponents. His initial teaching earned him hatred of the Pharisees and Herodians. However Comgall, unlike Jesus, was accepted as a prophet in his own land; the Irish Gaels of North Down welcomed the great saint.

In Jerusalem Christ enters into debate with the various representatives of the Jewish people; chief priests, scribes, elders, Pharisees, Herodians and Sadducees. Christ's death was brought about by the Jewish leaders in unity in crucifying the Messiah. Only the disciples could understand what it meant to be a follower of Christ. The role of the Virgin Mary in Christ's death and ministry is very important. An unnamed woman anoints Jesus, thus identifying him as the Messiah and preparing for his burial. Jesus had many followers in Galilee, and Comgall's Church had a place allotted for women in the service of God.

For Mark and Comgall Christianity meant that most of one's life was devoted to the service of Jesus. Christ's call had to be acknowledged and a personal relationship had to be struck up with the Creator. Comgall entered into communion with Christ's suffering. Christ had given up his life for the sake of the sins of all the world. The Scriptures had spoken; "Be watchful! Be alert! You do not know when the time will come". In the gospel according to Saint Matthew, the Old Testament plays an important role. It was written for a Jewish Christian community. It was first written in Hebrew or Aramaic, but it creates more problems than it solves. The text that has come down to us was perhaps composed in Greek in a place with a substantial Jewish population, probably in the east Mediterranean area. The most likely cities are Antioch in Syria, Damascus or Caesarea Maritima in Palestine. Matthew wrote about the destruction of Jerusalem, suggesting a date of composition around AD 85-90.

The evangelist is said to have produced a revised and expanded version of Mark's gospel. He also tried to help the Jews after the loss of Jerusalem. Matthew preached about the role of Christ in the economy of the Jewish faith. Comgall loved the five great speeches in the gospel of Mark. He also liked the sermon on the mount, the missionary discourses, the parables and the advice to the community. Perhaps Matthew is the most Jewish of the gospels. However it is claimed that Matthew could be anti-Jewish in his attitudes, for was not Christianity a final solution to the problems of the Roman Empire and of the world. The Book of Matthew may have been a reaction to Judaism under which Christianity grew up. Matthew, like the other disciples, regarded himself as a Jewish evangelist. Christ had come to fulfil the law and Matthew and his followers were there to carry out the word of God.

Christians observed the moral of the Old Testament, and the New Testament was there to fulfil the law, and to record the life of Christ. Comgall believed in the sovereignty of God, that it would be celebrated by all Creation. Matthew records that Jesus is the "Emmanuel", which means in Hebrew "God with us". Comgall was sure that Jesus would be with him always, "even unto the end of the world". Comgall learned from the Bible that he had to understand the sufferings of the community, both Christian and pagan. The Church at Bangor Abbey represented a community that was governed by the risen Christ. In the gospel of Matthew it is said that Peter was to be the leader of the Christian community. He was given the power to bind and loose.

Comgall had not recorded which of the gospels he liked best. Perhaps he loved each one on its merits. Unlike Saint Paul, Matthew knew the Messiah during his mission and so Comgall may have taken up the role of Saul or Paul just as he had evangelized the tribes and nations of the Mediterranean world. The author of Luke was apparently a Gentile

Christian with a good and lively knowledge of Judaism. He had shown how Christianity spread out from the eastern Mediterranean to Rome. The author may have been a Gentile who was attracted to Judaism without fully converting to Judaism. Luke seems to have been a co-worker with Saint Paul, and it is certain that he looked to Saint Peter (the first Pope?) for leadership at the imperial city. The same person may have written the Acts of the Apostles. Luke's gospel was composed about AD 85-90, and Luke explains why he wrote it and why he wanted to provide an orderly account of the career of Jesus and the early Catholic Church. Luke passionately describes the career of his master and accepts the fact of the empty tomb. Like the other disciples he may have seen apparitions of the Messiah, telling him to preach to the whole world, to set up the Catholic Church at Rome, and to accept Saint Peter as head of this persecuted religion. The gospel of Luke ends with the ascension of Christ into Heaven. Luke presents Christ as "the" figure in world history. His coming started a new system of dating (AD dating), that was established in the first half of the sixth century, just as Comgall was establishing himself in Ulster as a great preacher. In Luke there is special reference to the poor, women, tax collectors, sinners, and he urges the rich to do good to the poor. He prays nearly every moment of his life. Luke ends by saying that, "Then he took them out to the outskirts of Bethany, and raising his hands he blessed them. Now as he blessed them, he withdrew from them and was carried up into Heaven. They worshipped him and then went back to Jerusalem full of joy, and they were continually in the temple praising God".

John's gospel is different from the Synoptic Gospels. It says that Jesus's mission took place over a period of three years whereas the other gospels say that it may have taken only a year. John says that Jesus journeyed to Jerusalem several times, whereas other Scriptures record only one such journey. The nature of Christianity in John seems to be fundamentally different from the Synoptic Gospels. Again, it may be that the author attributed to in the Bible was in fact John or some other evangelical or missionary. The community that he wrote for were Jews in the process of being expelled from the synagogue. The Johnnine community lived in the eastern Mediterranean, perhaps Syria, Transjordan or Palestine. John's gospel seems to have taken shape between AD 90-100. John is full of the miracles associated with Christ and he totally believed in his Messiah, unlike Judas and Peter (who eventually asked for forgiveness) and took up the leadership of the infant Catholic Church. Jesus says farewell to his disciples and he washed their feet. John says farewell to his Christ, and celebrates holy communion, a fundamentalist or symbolic presence of the Body and Blood of Christ.

Chapter 17

Trade and Transport in Sixth Century Ulster

In the sixth century Ulster was a crazy quilt of bogs and moors. Comgall may have made the journey into the Antrim Hills, where there was plentiful turf; alternatively he may have travelled south east into the kingdom of Mourne and Dundrum Bay. How often he would have made these journeys is unknown, but they may have been frequent in view of the fact that he was evangelizing. In Antrim and Down Comgall met the local chiefs after travelling over the bogs and moorlands, but it is more likely that he travelled by ship along the coast of North Down, and into the Irish Sea, hugging the coast with his disciples in their currachs and landing perhaps in the present day Newcastle area. At Downpatrick he would have visited the graves of Saint Patrick, Saint Columba and Saint Brigit, said to have been buried together, a tribute to their lives spent evangelizing and a triumph for the Catholic Church. As we have seen in another chapter, there were highways, but these only served the main routes, e.g., Tara near Dublin to Dunseverick on the north coast of Antrim. Tara is a legendary place, but perhaps some sort of High-Kingship existed, for it is often referred to in the annals. Certainly it seems likely that Patrick had converted the High-King Laeghaire. We only rely upon the annals to create a picture of communications in sixth century Ulster. The monastic texts are also to be consulted. The roads followed high grounds and eskers, and they skirted the mountain sides, and fords were created at crossing points in rivers.

The highways are called slige in the literature. Slige is derived from the Irish word alijid which means "to fell", and which may have originally meant a roadway cut through woodland or made with felled timber. There were no rivers of any importance in North Down — the entire area seems to have been cultivated by the monks and their people. The abbey traded in livestock and goods in the same way as some secular organizations. To the west lay the River Bann in central Ulster; here crossings have been made according to the literature and in place names. Snáin was where water could be crossed by swimming, but of course the rivers were dangerous. Light plank bridges were thrown over rivers at various points and wet grounds were crossed by a tochar or timber causeway. There were various classifications of roads. The sét was a pathway or cattle track suitable only for travel on foot or on horseback. The bóthar was a droving road. Droving roads appear to be common, for cattle was a great measure of value in ancient Ulster. Many droving roads may have emanated from Bangor Abbey, serving the North Down community. Rót was the general roadway suitable for wheeled transport and fenced on each side with a ditch or a dyke. The ráinat was a main highway which passed by the residences of kings. The Gaels who travelled had the obligation of keeping the roads in good repair.

It took time to get from A to B in sixth century Ulster. The journey from Bangor Abbey to Tara perhaps took four or five days. The road from Tara to Dunseverick came into view of the spectacle of Rathlin Island. As far as transportation is concerned there were wagons; the wheeled cart, of the block wheel and other varieties drawn by horses or by sea was in general use for the carriage of goods. These were also used as hearses, and the chariot often mentioned in the saga literature seems to have been little different from the common cart. These carts may not have been used for long journeys. Possession of wheeled transport may only have been the luxury of the wealthy. The poor perhaps used carts that had no wheels to carry crops and other items. Most authorities seem to think that overland journeys into the heart of the land, in Central Down, were undertaken as a regular feature, but travel by water is also common; the currach or small skin-covered boat was used along the Down coast.

The inland rivers and small lakes were busy in their currach traffic. The currach could be taken out of the water and carried overland to the next stretch of water. Important places like the River Bann and Lough Neagh were alive with boats. To the south of Bangor Abbey lay the great stretch of Strangford Lough with its many islands, which was also the home of monks and anchorites. There is the monastery of Macha Island on the west shore. The dugout canoe (coite) of all sizes and dimensions, was in general use from the earliest times to the modern age, and was also used in times of war and for thieving and trade. This was the type of boat used mostly by thieves. Larger vessels were of course used in the broader waters or Belfast Lough. These vessels would sail to far away destinations like the Isle of Man, the coast of Britain and to Scotland (the Western Isles). The larger vessels were made out of wood, and were of various lengths. They were driven by the wind, and they made a colourful and romantic sight on the waters of Belfast Lough, the North Channel and the Irish Sea. The sailing time to Scotland took perhaps a day, and the longer journey to Britain took up more time.

There was perhaps a trade in cattle and livestock between the North

Down coast and these destinations. Certainly the monks of Bangor may have sailed north to the Western Isles to the monastery of Iona, Columba's great foundation and base for evangelizing the Picts of northern Scotland. It is not known how long it took to build one of these bigger ships, but the annals tell us that they would be used in warfare. Sea battles would take place in Belfast Lough between the monks of Bangor and pagan pirate vessels. Battles would also be waged in Lough Neagh, Strangford Lough and Lough Foyle in the north east of the province. It appears that intercourse between monasteries must have taken place by boat. Bangor would communicate with the monasteries of the south of Ireland. Many monasteries like Bangor, also communicated via the land, if the monastery was situated inland. Currachs were capable of carrying twenty monks or more. They were constructed with a wooden frame and covered with hides. It ranged in size from a small craft to larger boats. The larger ships were fitted with a keel and mast, sailyard sail and rigging. The monks and subjects of the rís sailed north to Iona and south to Devon and Cornwall, and even further afield to the coast of Spain and Portugal. The coast of North Down and Antrim was in continual contact with the cultures of the west of Scotland. News came back that there was a warlike race called the Picts (because they painted their bodies). They charged into battle. At a later date (sixteenth century) the Scots were to invade Antrim and Down, particularly subjecting the littoral, extending from Derry in the north west to the Mountains of Mourne in the south-east. There were battles between Antrim Dalriada and the other little kingdoms of the west of Scotland. It has not been clear how victorious were Comgall's monks. The High-King has been cited as having sailed into battle on the Irish Sea. He almost certainly sailed north to the coast of Down, making an appearance with the monks of the abbey. Also, there were alliances between the people of North Down and some of the other Irish kingdoms, as well as alliances with the tribes of eastern Britain, and that of the Isle of Man. It is not certain to what extent the abbey and the small kingdoms traded with each other. The histories and annals of the abbey perhaps recorded the trading that was carried on between North Down and other places, but this has, like other things, been lost to history. There was an internal trade in manufactured articles, or at least in raw materials. Some objects have been recovered from the ground — iron for weapons, stone for querns and whorls in other parts of Ireland. The same must hold true of the North Down and Bangor area. There must have been some network of distribution however simple, for imported goods. Foreign trade seems to have been great in the sixth century, and the abbey must have made a lot from a variety of manufactures.

The earliest map of Ireland, that of Ptolemy, is a trader's map, based on information gleaned from merchants. The abbey may have traded as far away as East Rome and its capital Constantinople — certainly the monks would have heard of this golden capital and its great wealth. The Roman Tactitus declared that the harbour and approaches to Eirinn were well known to traders. Gaulish merchants went as far north as Iona in Scotland. Other sources say that merchants made their way up the River Bann and the Foyle, trading with the tribal kingdoms. Of course they must have reached as far south as Tara, seat of the High-King Kingship, near the east coast of Ireland. The merchants reached the interior of the country, that lived independently from the other Irish confederate tribes. It has been pointed out that there were Gaulish market places in the centre of Eirinn. The merchants sold their wares and the monks of Bangor as well as celebrating mass with wine, also believed that a little wine was good for one's stomach's sake, according to the teaching of Jesus. Merchants may have called at Bangor trying to sell Comgall some wines. Other goods were sold — cargoes of iron, salt, hides, nuts, honey and the wine. They laid down provision for the landing of cargo ships. There are numerous references in the literature and histories for the import of wine, salt, iron and to the export of hides and wool.

Amber (orange) beads were also imported, probably from the east coast of England. The wine trade flourished high above the other sorts of commerce, and from the sixth century we can draw a picture of the average Irishmen as liking their drink. Comgall was a good Christian and a monk, and it is doubtful if he indulged himself excessively. How expensive wine was in ancient society is not known, but in ancient days when there were no clean water supplies, alcohol in bottles and vats was a necessity. The monks, along with Comgall may have drank wine or beer for breakfast, a situation that did not change with the coming of the Middle Ages. The medieval historian Geraldus Cambrensis writing in the twelfth century said that "Imported wine is so abundant that you would scarcely notice the vine was neither cultivated nor grown there". Wine therefore was imported and the hides of domestic animals and wild animals were exported. It is not known how these goods were distributed. Perhaps the ordinary Gael and customers came to the monks and bought goods. Alternatively the monks may have travelled widely with their produce. Certainly there was a great demand for wine. There may have been trading posts throughout the North Down area. The monks traded with the Belfast region and they would travel east to Donaghadee and south to Downpatrick.

There were other monasteries which the monks traded with. There is some uncertain knowledge of markets, and it is probable that imported goods, which were luxuries, were sold directly to their customers. The monastic system was superior to lay administration; the agricultural system of the monks was also superior, and with the monks came the faithful. They were in a position to develop a surplus in their economy far quicker than the kings and the tribal regions. To trade of course was not contrary to the law of God, in fact Christianity encouraged the money and capitalist

H

system as well as endorsing the spiritual activities of the faithful. There were famines and rumours of wars, and the abbey's economy was geared to warlike activities, despite this being contrary to the Scriptures. In times of great plague the kings robbed and sacked the monasteries, a general sacking that took place during the Reformation at a much later date. There was also cattle plague. By the eighth and ninth centuries, monastic towns with streets emerged (occasionally paved), a process that had been afoot since Comgall's days. Small towns soon developed in the great monastic farm lands, an important feature of the Irish economy. The secular rulers tried to take over the monasteries. A great foundation like that of Bangor competed with the secular powers for the tribal regions were small in comparison to monastic spheres or parucias.

It is likely that the monks tried to imitate European methods of trade, for was not Europe one big happy family ruled by the Pope. The Ulster economy was coinless in comparison to the Anglo-Saxon kingdoms in Britain. Comgall lived in a world of barter. He accepted cattle and other produce for celebrating mass, and accepted it for the forgiveness of sins. This is not to say that Comgall was not aware of the many systems of the other European kingdoms. Europe inherited the coin society from the Roman Empire, and it is surprising that in the sixth century, Ireland was a coinless confederacy of tribes. At Armagh the archbishop was in possession of coins, and the Church may have realized that coins would eventually take their place in Ireland.

In the classical law tracts the unit of value and exchange is the sét which was the equivalent of a heifer or half a milk cow. The largest unit of value was the cumal, originally meaning a bond woman, but normally used as the equivalent of two séts. Fines, compensations of general values are reckoned in this clumsy currency. There was also the system of exchange and of reckoning values in silver and bullion. An ounce of silver was the basic unit of the system. The silver ounce is frequently equated with the sét but this was valued in accordance with market fluctuations and its value was therefore changed from time to time. In the law tracts we find that a cow was worth two silver ounces. If the Vikings had reached Ulster as early as the fourth century, they would have come across the barter economy. By the sixth century the Viking system had become established as monasteries like that of Bangor were sacked and the valuables stolen. Some Roman coins have been discovered in Ireland, chiefly at the sea ports.

The Romans had a sophisticated system of communications, both on land and sea, and this far outstripped the Irish roads along which Patrick, Columba and Comgall travelled on their missionary journeys. Like the Romans the Irish had the use of wheels, which were used to carry out their business by means of carts and other systems of transport. The medicine man also took advantage of the Gaelic roads, and there was quite a sophisticated system of medicine in the country. This was folk medicine. As in the modern age the best system of medicine was based upon reassurance and before the days of modern medicine, the system was very important. At Bangor, a well blessed to a saint was a source of healing. There was also the use of charms, but eighty per cent of the Gaels went away without any form of treatment. Modern medicine treats such illnesses as cancer and other life threatening conditions. In Ulster in the sixth century, herbs were used as cures, whereas modern medicine relies on drugs. Also one third of any people seeking medical advice had nothing physically wrong with them. There are the imaginary conditions where illness has been brought about by tension, for example peptic ulcers, asthma, some skin diseases, colitis, many cases of high blood pressure and thyrotoxicosis. If these conditions are not treated, death may intervene. A herb doctor was just as likely to achieve success with such patients as a modern doctor. In sixth century Ulster treatment was expensive. A doctor might be attached to a great figure like Comgall, who like Jesus perhaps claimed he could cure illness by an act of faith.

In the past qualified doctors were few and expensive, so that only the rich consulted them, but this may not have excluded the monasteries. Usually there was a local healer. They could diagnose such illnesses as jaundice, but there again the illness might go away without treatment. The doctor would therefore get the credit for an illness that would go away anyway. In some cases credit was given to the unqualified practitioners, the hereditary bonesetters, some of whom still practise in some parts of Ireland. Unofficial medicine was widely practised. Many of the men and women that practised unofficial medicine were quite sincere and believed in the effectiveness of their treatment, and a few were given large amounts of money for it. Presents were sometimes given to them and in many cases money was refused. It is difficult to find the origins of such cures; many seem to have been derived from official medicine. However disorders of the nervous system nearly always went untreated and perhaps magic was called upon. As in modern medicine there were the quacks, and today folk medicine has declined. In Comgall's day the ultimate doctor was Christ and his Bishop of Rome. Christ had cured illnesses just in the same way that the druids of North Down had performed miracles and magic.

Chapter 18

The Sacraments

According to the Roman Catholic Church there are seven sacraments — Baptism, Confirmation, the Holy Eucharist, Penance, Anointing of the Sick, Sacred Orders and Holy Matrimony. The sacraments lie at the heart of the faith that Comgall held. It is through the sacraments that Christ has revealed himself to Comgall. It is likely that the early Church held as canonical many of these sacraments, which brought life into the commandments of the Catholic Church.

The mystery of the sacraments are part of God's plan for his people, and he confided often with very special followers and saints like Comgall. According to Tertullian, a great doctor of the Latin Church, Christ was immersed in the waters of the River Jordan by John the Baptist. When Christ spoke he spoke to the spiritually thirsty and he walked on water. Upon Calvary he was given a taste of water as his Passion unfolded. Now water is used to baptize infants and converts to the Roman Catholic Church. Pilate washed his hands in relation to Christ's death. Pierced by his side blood and water flowed from the Messiah. Baptism was the gateway to Christ for Comgall, and upon immersion rests the efficacy of the other six sacraments.

The word "baptism" derives from the Greek baptisei which means to "immerse" or to "plunge". By baptism sins were washed clean and a contract was established with God. It is not clear where Christ instituted baptism. Some authorities think that he may have instituted it at the time of his baptism by John the Baptist. For Comgall the idea of baptism was an evolutionary process — the baptism introduced by Christ and the baptism as it was held by the fathers of the Church, also an evolutionary process. Jesus sent his apostles out to baptize, and the origins of baptism may go back to these times. Comgall's Church seems to have been in conformity with the Roman Church on baptism — "John I baptize you in the name of the Father, and of the Son, and of the Holy Spirit". The ordinary minister of baptism is a bishop, a priest or a deacon and the recipient of course may not have already been baptized.

Baptism brought Comgall's converts into communion with God and of course membership of the Church. Baptism was essential for salvation, but surely a liberal like Comgall must have taken into account those that have not heard the word preached by Christian preachers. There was the question of infants that died without receiving baptism, and it seems that the fundamentalist believed that these infants could not be part of the Church's plan for mankind. The number of sacraments in the Church was also a progressive phenomenon. Protestants (Anglicans) today claim that there are only two sacraments — baptism and holy communion (the Eucharist). Pope Pius XII said in "Justic Corpros" that "By the chrism of Confirmation new strength is infused into believers that they may uphold and defend vigorously the Church, their mother and the faith, which they have received from her".

Confirmation is the second sacrament. Comgall learned and taught that confirmation is an essential sacrament, for baptism and confirmation are linked to each other. The initiated are reborn the sons of God. Confirmation consisted of two rituals — a laying on of hands and an anointing with perfumed oil called chrism. Confirmation can be traced back to the Old Testament, but Catholic confirmation is the result of Jesus's teaching and the teaching of the Church fathers. Confirmation gave grace to the recipient. The Church fathers tell us that confirmation was brought about by the laying on of hands, this ceremony usually carried out by a bishop. This laying on of hands was accompanied by anointing. Comgall may have wrote down that confirmation, like baptism, was essential for salvation and baptism was essential if one wanted to be converted and accepted into the Church of Rome. However the term "confirmation" was used for the first time at the convent of Rvez in AD 439, a century before the advent of Comgall and contemporary with Saint Patrick. One thousand years later the Irish Church witnessed the Papacy declare that confirmation was a sacrament and that it had existed since the foundation of the Church. The doctrine of confirmation can be traced back to the acts of the disciples and apostles, and it was usually performed by the anointing of the young or old Christians. Confirmation ensured that Christians set out along the righteous path. The bishops said that, "I anoint you with holy oil in the name of the Father, in Jesus Christ and in the Holy Spirit". Prayer accompanied confirmation, for prayer was and is the foundation of all those who want to believe. The Bible does not specifically point to the existence of confirmation. Confirmation appears to be the brainchild of the Latin Church, accepted by numbers of souls and converts like Saint Comgall. In the West however confirmation might be administered under special circumstances by a priest. There are some Christian denominations today that consider confirmation and other sacraments as the work of the Antichrist, for it is sufficient to believe in a power higher than oneself in order to be religious and good. However confirmation does not seem to be an act of Christian maturity, for confirmation like many other doctrines was implicit in the original revelation of Christ and has now become explicit in the life of the Catholic Church. The Church of Rome teaches today (and Comgall surely believed) that confirmation is essential for salvation.

In the Catholic Church the Eucharist is the central event in the history of the organization, and Pope John Paul II has stated that "It is at one and the same time a Sacrifice-Sacrament, a Communion-Sacrament and a Presence-Sacrament". Christ had called his disciples together on the eve of his passion at Calvary. He spoke about the role of the Messiah and how his followers should remember him. Christ was about thirty when he was crucified, and he had been preaching from the age of sixteen. The disciples must have known that their Messiah was going to his death. Certainly Christ himself must have realized this. He wanted his friends and apostles to celebrate the last supper with bread and wine as a celebration and declaration of faith. There were twelve apostles gathered about him as he celebrated the last supper or holy communion. The Catholic Church in its infancy and middle age has debated whether Christ meant a symbolic sacrifice or that transubstantiation had talen place. Perhaps Christ really meant that the wine was turned into the blood and the bread into the body of the Messiah. Comgall would have grown up on the Latin beliefs, i.e., that the Eucharist was a real sacrifice and that one was eating the bread and drinking the wine of the new covenant. The gospels are vague about the institution of the Roman Catholic Eucharist. They merely record a gathering together of apostles.

It appears that holy communion is an evolved doctrine, something that Christ might have endorsed as he went about his earthly mission. Perhaps the Church of Ireland (Anglican) is closest to the truth about what Christ meant at the last supper. He said, Comgall understood, that he was making a sacrifice, once and for all — his mission would end at Calvary, and he would ascend into Heaven to sit upon the right hand of the Father. However today the Roman Catholic Church clings to the traditional idea that Christ was continually making a sacrifice in the celebration of the Eucharist. The Catholic Church states that Christ had addressed his disciples and had said, "Take this, all of you, and eat it; this is my Body which will be given up for you". Over the chalice the words are "Take this, all of you, and drink it; this is the cup of my Blood, the blood of the new and everlasting Covenant. It will be shed for you and for all, so that sins may be forgiven. Do this in memory of me".

The Greek Orthodox Church on the other hand does not believe in transubstantiation, but it also recognizes that Jesus at the last supper may have meant something more than a remembrance or celebration. In the

Roman Catholic Church, in Comgall's Ulster, the Church celebrated a Eucharistic communion. Comgall taught his followers that it was essential for renewal and belief that transubstantiation should be recognized and practised. The congregation of the faithful celebrated their faith as the Roman and Gaelic priest turned the water and bread into the body and blood of Jesus Christ. The Church has said about penance that "Without Christ the Church can forgive no sins without the Church". The entire history of Ulster bears witness to violence and hated in society that can only be forgiven by devout souls. Adam and Eve had to have their sins forgiven after Adam had eaten the apple in the Garden of Eden. In this case it was up to God to forgive Adam and Eve and to drive them out of the Garden of Eden. At this point they knew shame, but they mated with each other, bearing children.

Adam and Eve, forgiven by Christ, founded the human race. One had to obtain forgiveness of sins in this life in order to enter Heaven, and the human race had to die to return to dust, unlike Adam and Eve who supposedly had eternal life bestowed upon them by God. Comgall had accepted most of the Latin Church's doctrines and dogmas in relation to sin. The idea of penance is typified in the parable of the prodigal son. The son went into a far country and spent his inheritance and he returned to his father, who forgave him. He stretched out his arms to the fallen relation, accepting him back into his home. Also, Saint Peter had the power to forgive, for he could "bind and loose", carrying out God's will on earth. For the ordinary Gael in sixth century Ulster it was sufficient to obtain forgiveness of sins from a priest. Comgall of course was a great forgiver of sins and he daily must have heard confession from his monks, who may have sinned only in small ways. Christ forgave the human race for its sins by the act of dying on the Cross, and his mother Mary could also help in the forgiveness of sins, for she was a great mediator in the Church.

The fathers of the Church had also forgiven sins and they have left a rich literature. Comgall has been remembered as one of the great Gaelic fathers, and he takes his place alongside Saint Patrick and Columba. Comgall was sure that all sins could be forgiven, whilst other Catholics believed that a righteous life was essential in order to reach Heaven. Saint Paul was also a great forgiver of sins and he forgave sins in the name of the Church. The average Gael obtained forgiveness for the slightest transgressions, and Comgall taught them that penance was one of the great sacraments. Today the Protestant Churches disagree with the Church of Rome over the number of sacraments, but all are agreed that only God can forgive sins. The Catholic Church however teaches that Mary, Christ's mother had a role to play. Only the priest could forgive sins in the name of Christ, no matter how serious these sins may have been. An act of penance brings about forgiveness, and this is one of the basic teachings of the Church, that she had the power to forgive and to bring about renewal.

The anointing of the sick is one of the most important sacraments of the Catholic Church. To reach Heaven it is essential to receive the sacraments. The anointing of the sick is peculiar to the Catholic Church and not to the Protestant denominations with the exception perhaps of the Anglican communion. That man has to die can be traced back to Adam and Eve in the Garden of Eden. Man does this so that he can be resurrected again if he has led a good life. However there is no biblical precedent for the anointing of the sick. The doctrine relies purely on the beliefs of the Latin and Greek Church Fathers. Comgall realised that sickness was bound up with man's fallen condition. Each Gael had to confess his shortcomings on his deathbed. In the Old Testament sickness is often identified with sin. The apostles and historians of the Old Testament tell about sickness and how death had to be faced. In Saint James in the New Testament we learnt that "If one of you is ill, he should send for the elders of the Church, and they must anoint him with oil in the name of the Father, and pray for him". The prayers of faith will raise him up. If he has committed any sins he will be forgiven. Anointing of the sick has not received the same publicity as the other sacraments like that of penance. Anointing of the sick took place in private whilst penance was a more public affair. Comgall exhorted his followers and other Gaels to observe the anointing of the sick at death.

The oil used in the anointing is derived from the olive, but animal or mineral oil cannot be used. A priest can bless the oil, if a bishop's blessing cannot be obtained. Under the present procedure the sick person is anointed on the forehead and the palms of the hands. By custom a priest is anointed on the back rather than on the hands because of the previous anointing at ordination. Anointing of the sick takes place when the priest regards his parishioner close to death. The recipient knows that he is close to death and wants to make his peace with Christ. As with Comgall, as death approached, the Christian communicant looks back at his life and makes an ultimate confession with the act of anointing. With a deathbed confession the followers of Comgall can be let through the gates of Heaven to be received by Jesus as a good Catholic. The act of anointing is the uniting of the sick person to the Passion of Christ, for his own good and that of the whole Church. Undoubtedly the seven sacraments, particularly the anointing of the sick are continually received and debated by the Church of Rome.

The sixth sacrament is sacred orders. Priests and presbyters are mentioned in the Bible, but not archbishops or popes. Christ is depicted as a king and not a prime minister or a president. However from their beginnings in the New Testament, the primitive Christians must have agreed that there should be some sort of authority to which monks like Comgall could look to in order to safeguard their faith. This original authority, the Catholic Church teaches, is the Pope, the cardinals, archbishops, bishops, priests and presbyters. Did Christ himself ordain that the Church should have an earthly head, for as we have seen Saint Peter arose with executive authority not only in this world but the next. Saint Paul presumably led the Catholic Church along with Saint Peter and the other apostles, but at Rome they are said to have met their death for the sake of the Church.

The Church teaches that once a man is invested as a priest that he is always a priest, and he still has the power to celebrate holy communion. The faithful march along the road to Calvary with the persecuted Christ. Comgall however was a monk, and not a priest, but monasticism can also be traced back to the ancient Church for was not John the Baptist an anchorite who lived in the desert, where he would become closer to God? Monks and nuns were essential for the smooth running of the wheels of the Catholic Church, a tribute to the life of Saint Comgall.

The seventh sacrament is holy matrimony, a state that can be traced back to the Garden of Eden, when man and woman were made for each other, even though they had eaten the apple of the tree of knowledge. Matrimony was also common to other civilizations and cultures, and polygamy was very often the rule. The Catholic Church taught that a man should have only one wife, and that divorce was only granted in exceptional circumstances. The original man and woman had been placed in the Garden of Eden by God, and they went about naked, knowing no shame.

When the apple was eaten the earthly state of matrimony came into existence. The New Testament — and Jews — praised the state of marriage between a man and a woman, but matrimony seems to have been introduced for the purpose of procreation, its foundation being the love that man had for woman, in a state of holy matrimony. During the first century many married Christians chose death rather than bow down to the Roman imperial system. Most of the apostles however seem not to have been married and Christ had ordained that the state of celibacy was superior to the state of holy matrimony. Christ himself was not married, but he must have been loved by many women, for he was the Messiah loved by his mother Mary, later to be loved by the Churches as the mother of God. There was therefore a place for many nunneries that grew up in Ulster, in the wider field of Ireland and on the continent of Europe.

Chapter 19

Learning and Literature

In Ulster the concept of the poet (fili) and of poetry (filidecht) dated back into antiquity and differed entirely from the modern concept of the poet, a creative man of literature. The word "fili" meant a seer, a wiseman and he competed with the druids or magicians for a place in sixth century Ulster society. The fili was therefore a man to be admired for his learning and powers of knowledge. At the dawn of the historical period, the poets were a powerful privileged class, and they claimed like the druids that they had magical powers. They guarded the ancient traditions (senchas) which included tribal and dynastic origin legends, mythology, tales of imagination and genealogy. They were the most important persons attending a royal inauguration, to which they conveyed kingship to the new king. They wrote praises to the new king, conveying the external signs of righteousness and justice. They were great satirists and they ranked equal to Comgall's Christian followers in their attitude to society.

The poets were also the guardians of the traditional tales. The fili appear to have been opposed to Christianity, but Comgall's sixth century Gaelic Church had included many pagan ideals and tracts against the heresies. Irish literature of the sixth century produced a rich blend of ecclesiastical and native learning. The pagans read Comgall's versions of the Scriptures, that is those who could read and write. They learned of the ancient form of Judaism that had taken root in the near eastern deserts and along the Mediterranean shores, a faith that took root in Egypt, now in the sixth century a province of East Rome. Comgall however respected the fili and the druids, but he was confident that they could be included in the Christian tradition. The pagans marvelled at the Christian copies of the Bible, and they had never seen a greater book, a book full of the acts of God in the Old Testament, and the acts of Jesus in the New Testament. The Bible was full of poetry and the monks of Bangor Abbey had memorized many verses, which they quoted in their missionary journeys in Ireland.

The Bible was a great work of literature, read widely throughout the ruins of West Rome and in the high society of the Byzantine Empire of East Rome. Now the High-King of Tara, the Irish confederate emperor, had copies brought to him from the great monasteries of Ireland, and Bangor must have been one of the most important schools. Comgall was absorbing the pagan tradition for he was aware that the Church had to meet the pagans half way, as long as the Ten Commandments were not breached (we have already discussed the theory of images, where in East Rome icons were used to gain a knowledge of the faith).

The fili had expanded to include separate castes of lawyers, poet-historians and praise poets. The Brehon laws or Gaelic laws were the preserve of a legal caste. Unlike the tribal kingdoms of sixth century Britain, the Gaelic lawyers wrote nothing down. These laws were at length written down in the seventh century, or perhaps in the sixth century. Once written down, the laws had to be interpreted, a process which took at least a century to complete. Later still the tracts took the form in which we now have them. The most outstanding book is the Senchas Mór, an eighth century phenomenon. For the experts the laws were unchangeable, rather like the system of doctrines and dogmas of Comgall's Church. The preservation of the Senchas, traditional historical law, always remained the preserve of the poets. They were the custodians of Irish mythology, origin legend, genealogy, king lists and synchronism of the kings. Some fabrication has entered the law tracts, but generally they are quite historical. The law tracts grew up independently of the Tara High-Kingship for other abbeys like Bangor Abbey enjoyed an independence of central authority.

The law affected the ordinary Gael of North Down and of Ulster/Ireland. The poetical sagas told of the evolution of many tribal kingdoms, e.g., the Dal Fitach kingdom of North Down. The process of writing down may have started in the sixth century or earlier. Comgall respected the pagan historians, and he may have drawn upon their wisdom as he preached the gospel. Comgall emerges as both an evangelist and an historical doctor of the Irish Church. Most of his Christianity was based upon the literal interpretation of the Bible demanded of him by the Pope. The Bible of course also included great poetry, as witness the Song of Songs in the Old Testament. In the New Testament Christ spoke in parables, a kind of poetry. The Ten Commandments are also poetical and inspired the Gaels of Down. However the importance of the ordinary man in the sixth century was measured in his line of descent, a knowledge of his genealogy was the preserve of the Gaelic historian. Comgall, it has been pointed out, in an earlier chapter could trace his line of descent to an early Gaelic family living in the Magheramourne region of the Laharna tribe in East Antrim. An old Irish text urges, "Memories shall determine to whom inherited land belonged: old antiquities shall be questioned truthfully ... let genealogical branches be extended when children are born". The writer was referring to the jurists. Genealogical material was also of high political consequence.

Dynasties ruled the North Down tribal area by virtue of their descent from ancient royal lineages (and possibly in pagan times from the tribal god of war). The work of the poet historian is not strictly speaking political for such genealogies reflect tribal ways as well as historical descent. When new kings rose up to claim the leadership of the tribe, his genealogist often forged a link between them and their predecessors and in this way continuity and legitimacy were assured.

It is not known to what extent the pagans of North Down contributed to the Christian ways of Comgall and his monks. Out of the historical tracts came the legends of the Ulster cycle, of Cuchullan and King Conor Mac Nessa of Armagh or Emain Macha. The Ulster cycle is a memorized tract and the poets and historians recited their own versions of it. Comgall also invited the historians into the abbey, and listened to the tales of ancient Ulster. The Middle Ages saw the histories and sagas being written down. However some of these date from the seventh and eighth centuries. Comgall wrote down all the Latin and Gaelic hymns, giving the Celtic Church a definite Gaelic character of its own.

By the end of the sixth century much that was good in paganism had been preserved by Comgall. He preached to the historians the values laid down in the Bible, particularly the gospels. The Old Testament however had its pagan points and virtues, and the Scriptures often refer to sin and the cities of Sodom and Gomorrah which were inspired by the Devil. To Comgall sin was synonymous with serious forms of paganism. The story of the Old Testament has as its theme man's struggle against sin and worshipping of the dark one. It is not known what parts of the Bible Saint Comgall liked best, but surely he was inspired, as we have seen, by Moses coming down from Mount Sinai with the Ten Commandments. The God of Israel was to be a spectacular God and was all loving and forgiving to his adherents.

The pagans came to love Christ as much as they loved their own gods. Comgall also read the New Testament and the story of Christ and as he now approached death, he may have loved the story of the resurrection. Like his great contemporary Saint Columba, Comgall started to look back upon his life, a life dedicated to the service of Christ and his virgin mother.

Comgall had had a long life, for this he thanked God, for his thoughts turned to the Book of Revelation and to his personal relationship with Christ. He may have died within the walls of his monastery, worshipped and loved by his fellow monks and the people of Ulster.

Chapter 20

Comgall and the Risen Christ

The wind was blowing around Bangor Abbey, and where it once stood we can sense Comgall's spirit. He looked back at his career as an evangelist. He had absolute faith in the spectacle of the risen Christ, and he had read over and over again Christ's missionary work in Palestine and the miracles that he had performed. Comgall had a very definite image of the crucified Christ. Christ had died for the sins of all the world, and Comgall was following in the footsteps of his master who had died over 500 years ago. To Christ this great saint prayed and to his mother the Virgin Mary. Comgall walked in the gardens of Bangor Abbey, talking with God, for Comgall knew that he was close to death, for he was now an old man. He had read the Book of Genesis, and believed that God had created the world and the Universe, in an age that believed that the world was flat. Comgall envisaged the Garden of Eden and Mount Sinai, where Moses had received the Ten Commandments, an eternal message for mankind. "Thou shall not kill" was perhaps the most difficult commandment that Comgall had to accept to follow in the footsteps of Christ. His eyesight was perhaps fading and he may not have been able to read the Scriptures. He had loved to read about the career of Jesus of Nazareth.

Comgall accepted the fact of the crucifixion and the risen Christ, this being central in his faith, for the crucifixion is the central event in the Church. Comgall celebrated mass, believing that the bread and wine were turned into the body and blood of Jesus. His monks must have known that the end was near for Comgall, and there were always younger monks in the abbey that would carry out Comgall's wishes. The saint may have had a healthy fear of death, but he was sure that God would judge him fairly.

God no doubt had dwelled within the walls of the abbey, he dwelt in the Dal Fitach kingdom of North Down with its many chapels. Comgall also went to this death accepting the leadership role of the Pope in the Catholic Church. He read the Book of Revelation and he believed that the second coming of Christ was drawing near. The Book of Revelation is hard to understand, and it is full of imagery quite suited to the beliefs of the Roman Catholic Church. In it the seer is granted a vision of a new earth and a new Heaven; it speaks directly from God, and is no ordinary work of literature. Its literary value is very important. It is a work of prophecy in which Comgall renews his faith not only in the Church, but also in Christ. The number "seven" is often mentioned in the Bible and this may have had a magical quality. Seven letters were given to the churches in Western Asia Minor (present day Turkey) in which he both praises and blames the individual communities.

Comgall's Christ was the historical biblical Christ, the Christ of the crucifixion, the Christ of the Virgin Mary and the Christ of the resurrection. This is what he had preached to the Gaels of North Down, who had come to love the frail saint. He had hated the Roman Empire in the East as a "pagan" organization, but looked up to it when it became Christian.

In his own eyes he was a great sinner, needing the love of God and the hope that this could bring him. He had at an earlier date come back from Pictland in northern Scotland where he had assisted Columba in the evangelization of the Picts. He started to walk around the grounds of the monastery many times. The sea was shining when Comgall looked out towards Carrickfergus and the Antrim Hills. He thought about Magheramourne, where he had been born, on the banks of Larne Lough. Perhaps he may have gone on a sentimental journey to Magheramourne, where the Gaels had been converted to the faith by his predecessor Saint Patrick. Ulster was left with a great father figure in Comgall, for Columba was resident at Iona and had no intention of coming home to live in Ulster. Comgall offered up his prayers, thinking of the risen Christ and his mother the Virgin Mary.

Hail, Holy Queen.

Select Bibliography

Adrian Fortescue, *The Early Papacy* (The Saint Austin Press, 1995)

Aidan O'Sullivan, *Crannogs* (County House, 2000)

Alfons Maria Cardinal Stiockler, *The Case For Clerical Celibacy* (Igatius Press, 1993)

Aongus Collins, *A History of Sex and Morals in Ireland* (Mercier Press, 2001)

Basil Hume (Cardinal), *The Mystery of the Cross* (Darton, Longman, Todd, 1998)

Carten Peter Thiede, *Heritage of the First Christians* (Lion Books, 1992)

Charlene Altmuse, *What You Should Know About Mary* (Liguori, 1998)

Daniel Harrington, *Revelation, the book of the Risen Christ* (New City Press, 1999)

Ian Adamson, *Bangor Light of the World* (Fairview Press, 1979)

J. N. D. Kelly (Editor), *Oxford Dictionary of Popes* (Oxford University Press, 1986)

Jacques Bar, *How to Understand the Virgin Mary* (SCM Press, 1976)

Liam Kelly, *Sacraments Revisited* (Darton, Longman, Todd, 1998)

Martin Wallace, *Celtic Saints* (Appletree Press, 1995)

Marian Kearney, *Celtic Heritage of Saints* (Veritas, 1998)

Martin Robinson, *Rediscovering the Celts* (Fount, 2000)

Olive Sharkey, *Ways of Old* (O'Brien Press, 2000)

Peter de Rosen, *Vicars of Christ* (Polbeg, 2000)

Patrick C. Power, *Sex and Marriage in Ancient Ireland* (Mercier Press, 1976)

Peter Beresford Ellis, *The Celtic Empire* (Robinson, 1990)

Paul Haftner, *The Sacramental Mystery* (Gracewing, 1999)

Patrick Logan, *Irish Folk Medicine* (Appletree, 1981)

Proinsias Mac Cana, *Celtic Mythology* (Chancellor Press, 1997)

T. G. E. Powell, *The Celts* (Thames & Hudson, 1963)

The Giant's Causeway (HMSO, 1992)

The New Jerusalem Bible (Darton, Longman, Todd, 1990)

The Bible, Revised Standard Version (The Bible Societies)